The French and Indian War

A Captivating Guide to the North American Conflict between Great Britain and France along with Its Impact on the History of Canada, the US, and the Seven Years' War

© Copyright 2022

All Rights Reserved. No part of this book may be reproduced in any form without permission in writing from the author. Reviewers may quote brief passages in reviews.

Disclaimer: No part of this publication may be reproduced or transmitted in any form or by any means, mechanical or electronic, including photocopying or recording, or by any information storage and retrieval system, or transmitted by email without permission in writing from the publisher.

While all attempts have been made to verify the information provided in this publication, neither the author nor the publisher assumes any responsibility for errors, omissions or contrary interpretations of the subject matter herein.

This book is for entertainment purposes only. The views expressed are those of the author alone, and should not be taken as expert instruction or commands. The reader is responsible for his or her own actions.

Adherence to all applicable laws and regulations, including international, federal, state and local laws governing professional licensing, business practices, advertising and all other aspects of doing business in the US, Canada, UK or any other jurisdiction is the sole responsibility of the purchaser or reader.

Neither the author nor the publisher assumes any responsibility or liability whatsoever on the behalf of the purchaser or reader of these materials. Any perceived slight of any individual or organization is purely unintentional.

Free Bonus from Captivating History (Available for a Limited time)

Hi History Lovers!

Now you have a chance to join our exclusive history list so you can get your first history ebook for free as well as discounts and a potential to get more history books for free! Simply visit the link below to join.

Captivatinghistory.com/ebook

Also, make sure to follow us on Facebook, Twitter and Youtube by searching for Captivating History.

Contents

INTRODUCTION 1
CHAPTER 1 - FIRST CONFRONTATION 4
CHAPTER 2 - THE "JUMONVILLE AFFAIR"..................................11
CHAPTER 3 - VENGEANCE VISITS FORT NECESSITY...............19
CHAPTER 4 - "YOU SHOULD HAVE FIRST ASKED OUR CONSENT" 31
CHAPTER 5 - WILDERNESS WAR 36
CHAPTER 6 - CANADIAN CAMPAIGNS BRING BRITISH VICTORY 51
CHAPTER 7 - THE "BLOODY" BATTLES SET THE STAGE IN NEW YORK..56
CHAPTER 8 - THE RULES OF BATTLE CHANGE 64
CHAPTER 9 - THE TRAGIC END OF FORT WILLIAM HENRY 71
CHAPTER 10 - THE BATTLE ON SNOWSHOES AND THE LEGEND OF ROGERS ROCK..87
CHAPTER 11 - A BRITISH VICTORY AND A HUMILIATING DISASTER 94
CHAPTER 12 - THE BRITISH TURN THE TIDE........................104
CHAPTER 13 - THE FALL OF QUEBEC AND THE "END" OF THE TRUE CANADA 114
CONCLUSION..124
HERE'S ANOTHER BOOK BY CAPTIVATING HISTORY THAT YOU MIGHT LIKE 127
FREE BONUS FROM CAPTIVATING HISTORY (AVAILABLE FOR A LIMITED TIME) 128
REFERENCES 129

Introduction

Two great empires, Britain and France, had a long-standing struggle for supremacy dating back to medieval times. The numerous battles and centuries' worth of conflicts caused bad blood to form between the powers, and aggressions began spilling over into colonial North America.

By 1756, the British and French had been fighting over imperial interests for two years. It caused plenty of tension over who had the rights to commercial trade, with many in government having a financial interest in the new land. But it was not just over the coveted trading of goods like beaver pelts. They also fought over alliances with native tribes. Each nation worked to woo allies away from the other. Threats flew from both sides, telling the other to back down or face dire consequences.

Native tribal leaders promised the British that they could build an outpost in the Ohio Forks region, but the French did not like this encroachment on what they considered their territory. They already held posts in Canada, New York, and Pennsylvania. Ohio was a strategic region for them, as it gave them a straight shot into their Louisiana territories. It would also serve to keep the British contained to the East Coast, making them unable to spread their armies and empire any farther west. The French worried that if a formidable British presence was allowed to grow on the continent, all of their colonies would fall. They were not wrong.

Tribal chiefs saw the trouble brewing between the British and French. For nearly a century, they managed to pit the two empires against each other and stay hidden in the shadows of war, coming out occasionally to fight. Despite having been able to maintain neutrality in the "white man's war" for so long, they now began to feel pressured to take sides. With more colonists arriving every year and the Europeans' hot ambition for land and its resources, they believed the survival of their people depended on it.

Some sided with the British, feeling that they were the greater military strength. However, most tribal leaders allied themselves with the French, as they appeared less land-hungry. The French also proactively wooed them with promises of "exotic" goods, liquors, and other luxuries, which they more often than not delivered on.

In addition to white settlers moving westward and pushing the Native Americans from their lands, tribes of the Iroquois Confederacy faced problems from within and from other indigenous nations. There were often conflicting interests, agendas, and allegiances, sometimes even within the same tribe. Western tribes moved into the Ohio Valley and farther eastward, trying to get closer to the white settlers with whom they could trade. This hemmed in the Iroquois tribes, like the Delaware and Shawnee, giving them few options.

The tribes were not the only ones caught between the two empires. Colonists, who were struggling to find freedom and survive in this new land, faced increasing difficulties as they were inevitably drawn into the conflict. This gave rise to bitter feelings about their home country.

This epic struggle between two empires would last from 1754 to 1763, but it stemmed from a larger war that began in 1756. The Seven

Years' War would spread across the globe. Though the French and Indian War was fought on North American soil, the conflict would have far-reaching consequences for many people. It would create new nations and change the course of world history forever.

Chapter 1 – First Confrontation

The major and his party had just ridden their horses fifteen miles on the cold morning of December 4th, 1753, the dampness of the rain the day before still hanging in the air. The log cabin he had so eagerly been riding toward now appeared, a white flag with a fleur-de-lis waving above. Major George Washington had finally arrived at the place where he would deliver an important message from Virginia Governor Robert Dinwiddie. It was his first mission of this kind, and his heartbeat quickened in anticipation.

The cabin, once a business and a home, had been fortified for defense by the trader John Fraser before he had been ousted by the French the year before. Leaving his native escorts to stay back, Washington took his translator and his field guide to the entrance of the cabin. There, three French officers and Captain Philippe-Thomas Chabert de Joncaire politely greeted the gentlemen and invited them in. He had heard much about the man on his journey, and now he stood in front of him, courteous to a fault toward sworn enemies.

Joncaire was born to a Seneca mother and a French father. He easily stood between the two worlds and held as much sway and influence in the region as any governor. He held a military position with the French, and he was also the chief interpreter for the Six Nations.[1]

Major Washington was eager to deliver his message from Dinwiddie. It was a letter demanding that the French remove themselves from these lands, as they were lands that the British declared they had already claimed. The French captain demurred. Although he replied that he was in charge of the Ohio region, he told the major that he really should bring this letter to the commander of Fort Le Boeuf another fifty miles away. The major was dismayed at having to ride such a long distance again the next day, but he accepted the captain's offer to eat with him and his officers. Though the two men with him stayed as well, the major had left the other Native Americans behind by design. He feared that the captain might somehow influence them.

As the dinner wore on, the Frenchmen drank wine freely, and tongues loosened. The French openly declared their intention of claiming the Ohio lands. Oh, they knew that the British would fight them for them, but they believed that the French would best them in the contest. The British, they confidently declared, were too slow to stop them. Besides, a Frenchman named La Salle had made it to the Ohio Forks region first. And now, Joncaire told them, the French were already chasing British families from their settlements, and they were determined to prevent any more from coming to the region under their control.

The major, who had remained perfectly sober, jumped at the opportunity to ply the inebriated Frenchmen for more information about their troops, supply lines, and forts. The French officers

---

[1] An Iroquois confederation council of fifty sachems (chiefs) from the Mohawk, Oneida, Onondaga, Cayuga, Seneca, and Tuscarora nations.

answered freely, seemingly unworried about the information they were letting loose.

The weather the next day prevented the party from riding out. Even if the weather had been favorable, by this time, Washington was now missing an important part of his party.

While the major and his men had been entertained by the French, the Seneca leader Half King and his men had visited their Delaware allies to hold council regarding the return of tribal treaty belts to the French.[2,3]

Half King had a deep hatred for the French for a number of reasons. When he was a boy, the French brutally murdered his father and dishonored his corpse afterward.[4] More recently, he had become bitterly resentful of the insolent and insulting treatment given to him by French Captain Pierre-Paul Marin de la Malgue. But his reasons for siding with the British were not strictly personal. With two large empires pressing in on the Six Nations' lands, it seemed unavoidable that sides would need to be chosen. The British seemed like the best of the two bad options available.

Half King had gone to Marin with a similar message as the British—leave the Ohio watersheds. But it was not due to an unwillingness to share the land and its resources. He told the Frenchman that the natives would have happily traded and lived beside the French settlers in the area had they been as friendly to them as the British had been.

---

[2] Tanacharison, or Half King as he was called by the British whom he had befriended, was a staunch and intelligent Seneca leader with a broad knowledge of the white men and their ways. The Six Nations' Grand Council appointed him as a leader and diplomat between the tribes, as well as a spokesman between the nations and the British. His leadership role earned him the moniker "Half King."

[3] Also called wampum or wampum belts, these articles made of strung-together white and purple clamshell beads held meaning and value. Wampum of different colors and styles held different meanings and were used for numerous purposes. In this instance, the return of the treaty belt meant that the agreement between the giver and the receiver was being terminated.

[4] He claimed that the French killed his father, boiled his body, and then ate it. The account is generally thought to be true.

Instead, the French had come and taken their land by force. Half King declared that the natives could not submit to this treatment. They officially called on the French to leave the area.

Marin told Half King that wampum or no, he would not listen to his words. He then referred to the natives as "flies or mosquitos," adding that he was afraid of neither. Marin continued, defiantly telling Half King that the French would indeed continue to build on the river. He practically dared the natives to try and oppose him. After flinging the wampum belt at Half King, he said the land belonged to the French and that no one had the right to say otherwise. Half King left the meeting with Marin incensed and offended.

Half King did not accompany the British in 1753 to reiterate his message to the other French commanders; rather, he looked for the support of the local tribes. He informed Delaware Chief Custaloga (also spelled as Kustaloga) that the "king" of the Delaware, Shingas, had ordered the tribe to return the treaty belt as well.[5] But Custaloga wanted to keep the peace and was reluctant to incite the French. He discovered a technicality through which he could refuse the order from his potentate. If Half King wanted to return the treaty belts to the French, he had to take the risk and do it without the Delaware tribe.

Once Joncaire got wind of the meeting that had occurred, he did exactly what Washington feared he would—he cordially invited Half King, White Thunder, and Jeskakake to his cabin for drinks, treating them as old friends and allies despite never having met them before. The men drank and drank, and not one word was uttered about the French leaving the valley.

Major Washington left in disgust. He knew exactly what game the French were trying to play, and he did not like it one bit. Joncaire was trying to win the native guides over to the French, and he was doing it

---

[5] Traditionally, the Delaware (also known as the Lenape) did not have kings. Shingas's brother had been named the "king" by the British, and when he passed away, the title went to Shingas.

right under his nose. The battle the French were fighting at the moment was one of diplomacy, and they excelled at it.

The next day, a sober Half King was determined to give his defiant "leave our land speech" to Joncaire. Washington tried to dissuade him, telling him he should wait to deliver the message to the fort commander. Really, though, he didn't care who heard the message; he just wanted to keep his native guides from further contact with the wily and persuasive Joncaire. However, he lost the argument, and Half King proceeded with the formalities.

After Half King's speech, Joncaire politely refused the wampum belt and told the native men to present it at the fort. But Joncaire was not about to end his bid to win over the natives. Washington's frontiersman guide, Christopher Gist, wrote that "Joncaire did everything he could" to get the natives to stay behind with the French. If he succeeded, it would be a huge blow to Washington, who relied on Half King not just to help him navigate the landscape but also in helping him navigate relations with the numerous tribes in the area.

That night, the major, his men, and four French escorts rode out toward the fort, joined by their four native companions whom they narrowly missed losing as allies. After four days of riding, the men arrived at Fort Le Boeuf.

Major Washington and his men were politely received and presented Governor Dinwiddie's letter to the fort commander, a tough Canadian named Jacques Legardeur de Saint-Pierre. It was to be the first formal confrontation between the British and French during this period. The message that Washington delivered announced to the French that it was a well-known and established fact that the lands around the Ohio River belonged to Great Britain. As such, the British Crown was surprised to find the French building forts and settlements there. Dinwiddie requested that the French leave in a peaceful manner.

While waiting for a reply, as the letter had to be translated into French, the major and his men took the time to inspect the fort, the barracks, and even the number of canoes the French had, taking notes so they could report their findings when they got back to Virginia. By the time they completed their inspection, the French had a reply and invited Washington to discuss it civilly over some wine. Despite all the courteousness, the answer was not appealing to the British. The Ohio River did not belong to the British but to the French, and the British did not have any right to use the waters for trading. In fact, any Brit caught doing so would be arrested. The French were prepared to defend their territory.

The French then tried to compel the major to bring his letter to the governor of Quebec, but Washington had grown tired of being bounced from one French commander to another. Besides, Legardeur had already given his answer, and Quebec was just another deflect and delay tactic. Washington wanted to allow Half King to have his say and then leave as quickly as possible.

But the French at Fort Le Beouf continued the same diplomatic battle that Joncaire had started. Though the French tried to put off hearing Half King, he was finally able to gain a private audience with the fort's captain. When the native leader tried to return the wampum belt to Legardeur, he refused it, declaring that he wanted to continue good relationships and trading with the natives.

If Half King found this refusal offensive, Legardeur was sure to make up for it by giving the Native American men every consideration. He knew how important Half King was as a path to gaining an alliance with the Six Nations, so he continued to employ crafty delay tactics in hopes of winning new allies and taking them away from the British. The French openly and unabashedly used the promise of liquor, guns, and other gifts in a brazen attempt to woo the natives away from the British, and it nearly worked. It gave George Washington some of the worst anxiety of his life, as he did not know whether he would lose his native allies that were so important to his current mission and the British cause.

The return trip, which took place in late December, was cold and snowy. The icy trails and difficult conditions strained their horses. Frostbite set in, rendering three of the men helpless. Yet the major was determined to get the French commander's answer back to Virginia without delay.

Not wanting to be held back by the ailing men and the wait for fresh horses, Washington took a backpack and had Gist follow him on foot. They trekked through the woods, even though it went against Gist's sage advice. A frontiersman like Gist had no trouble making the trek, but Washington was a gentleman and had difficulties. Their progress was slow.

The journey back was fraught with dangers and harrowing experiences. A native guide they picked up along the way tried to shoot them, narrowly missing both men. Half-frozen rivers with broken ice had to be perilously crossed using a hastily constructed raft that the men made using timber they cut down with a hatchet. Rough conditions caused Washington to fall out of his raft into the frigid waters, barely clinging on as Gist pulled him up. The men were unable to navigate the raft to shore, so Gist and Washington were forced to spend a freezing, ice-encased night on a small island. They then moved through the same woods where French Ottawa tribesmen had recently murdered and scalped an entire family.

Finally, on January 16th, 1754, one month after he left Fort Le Beouf, Major George Washington reached Williamsburg, Virginia. He was eager to hand in his reply and also report that the French were planning a seizure of the Ohio Valley, most likely in the spring. There was no time to waste.

Chapter 2 – The "Jumonville Affair"

Governor Dinwiddie frowned, dismayed as he read the letter. The French commander had written that he was not obliged to leave Ohio as the British had commanded. According to him, they had committed no acts of hostility toward the British, nor were they in violation of any treaty or trade agreement.

Dinwiddie was disappointed yet remained resolute. He saw the bigger picture and agreed with Washington that speedy action was paramount to their overall success. Preparations were made for the major to return to the Ohio Valley with a contingent of militiamen, including traders familiar with the Native Americans of the region.

That was easier said than done. Few voluntarily enlisted or were inclined to comply with the demands to muster. Angry, Dinwiddie began to invoke penalties on those who refused, hoping to motivate others to fall in line. Meanwhile, reports from native allies came in, telling of four hundred French reinforcements that were on their way to Ohio. Time and the ability to secure the Ohio Valley were rapidly slipping away.

Meanwhile, Dinwiddie ordered Captain William Trent back to Ohio to build a small stockade fort near the forks, which ensured the British continued to stake their claim to the area. Dinwiddie knew this was sure to provoke the French, but he would play this dangerous game nonetheless.

By March, Major Washington had three hundred unruly, undisciplined, and nearly ungovernable militiamen at his disposal. There was a promise that one thousand Native Americans would meet up with them. As much as these numbers might look sufficient, they did not tell the true picture. Some of the men had been released from prison just to join up. Many were without even the most basic supplies, including shoes or clothing, let alone guns. But they were all Washington had. He would have to make do.

Major Washington was also handed a commission that he had longed for—a promotion to lieutenant colonel and the assignment to finish building the British fort in Ohio that Captain Trent had started. With the minimum number of preparations now made, Lieutenant Colonel George Washington and his men set out for Ohio in mid-April 1754. After the treacherous Appalachian crossing, Captain William Trent raced to the party on horseback, delivering urgent news.

Upon opening the letter, Washington was delivered a shock—eight hundred French troops were about to descend on the unfinished British fort in Ohio. An attack was expected at any moment. Back in January, the native allies of the French had warned Governor Michel-Ange Duquesne about the British incursion, and they immediately began preparations to expel them from the lands. When the British came, the French were ready and waiting.

Since the small British column was still in West Virginia, there was no way they could make it in time to save their compatriots! Washington tried once again to hasten their journey, but slow wagons, the unavailability of horses, and lack of supplies made for an agonizingly sluggish pace. Just two days after Trent had delivered his news, another report was delivered on April 22nd. It confirmed the commander's worst fears—the unfinished fort had been taken by the French. Control of the fort meant control of the Ohio Forks. The British had lost before they had even begun.

Ensign Edward Ward, the messenger, was able to give an eyewitness account of what had happened. With Captain Williams away and Lieutenant Fraser indifferent to his duties, Ward became the senior officer of the forty-one soldiers guarding the unfinished fort. Upon hearing that the French were on their way, he enlisted the help of Half King and other natives, who advised a wooden stockade be built.

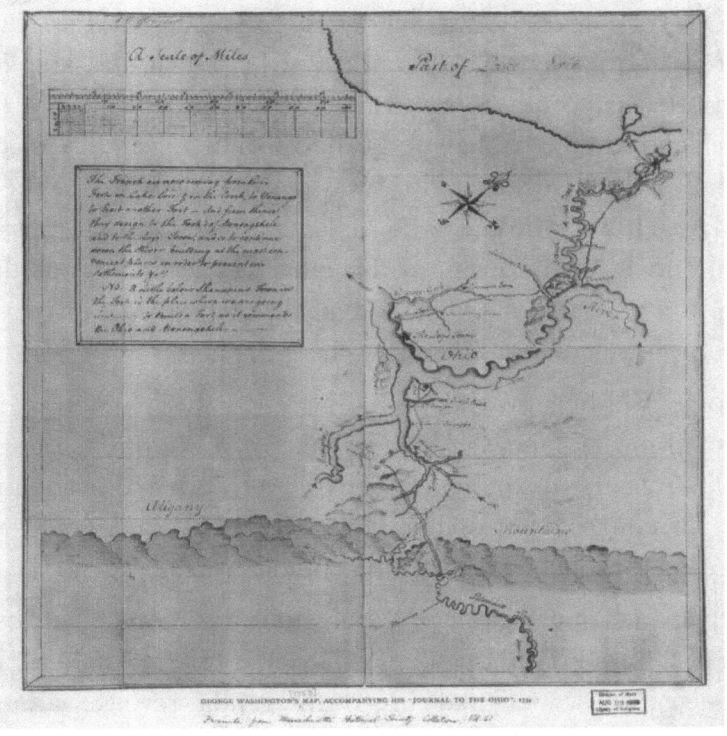

Map accompanying Washington's journal courtesy of Library of Congress.

https://commons.wikimedia.org/wiki/File:Gwash_map01.jpg

On April 17th, as the last gate was finished, the French arrived by canoe. They demanded that the British surrender immediately and leave with all of their belongings. Doing otherwise would have dire consequences for the outnumbered Brits.

With about one thousand French soldiers to his forty-one men, Ward had no choice but to leave. As they marched out, an angry Half King shouted to the French that the fort had been built on his authority and that he had laid the first post. He might be walking out at the moment, but for him, this wasn't over.

After Ward related his story, he handed the letter to Washington. In the letter, the French accused the British of disrupting the peace and harmony of the region when all the French wanted was to be able to use the area for trade.

The second letter Ward handed over was from Half King. He implored his old friend to come to their aid against the French, stating, "If you do not come to our assistance now, we are entirely undone, and I think we shall never meet together again. I speak with a heart full of grief." Tanacharison was greatly angered over the whole fort affair. He was the one who had made the decision to back the British, and he had convinced the other chiefs that it was the best option. But now, it looked like he had chosen poorly. For the sake of his honor, he needed to win against the French.

George Washington was grim. Even with native reinforcements, how could the 159 men he had left take on 1,000 French, especially given his military inexperience? There were a few other companies within marching distance, but they were weak and could not be counted on for much. The situation could hardly be worse.

Yet, Lieutenant Colonel Washington was compelled by Half King's plea for help, although he perhaps did not fully understand that the indigenous leader had his own agenda—revenge against the French. A victory would also help strengthen his position with his own people, as it would prove he had made wise decisions.

After strategizing, Washington decided to station his company at the British-fortified storehouse at Red Stone Creek and hold out for reinforcements. Hopefully, he would receive more commissioned officers because, up until then, he was sorely lacking those in his militia. He sent Ward and an escort of natives back with letters to Dinwiddie. He also sent messengers to Half King to meet with him to strategize.

The young commander had a lot on his plate. In writing to Dinwiddie, he expressed his concern, telling the governor, "Upon the whole, I find so many clogs in the expedition that I quite despair of success."

To add to his troubles, Trent met up with Washington's column with a group of militia volunteers he had raised. That would have been good news except that these hardscrabble traders were idle, greedy, and unable to be reasoned with. However, some of their protests for better pay were not without merit. But after a few days, Washington needed to separate them from his own men. They left in a huff, scattering and going about their own business. It was more of a relief than anything.

On May 24th, while waiting for reinforcements to take back the stolen fort, Washington set up camp at Great Meadows on a place he called a "charming field for an encounter." Chilling reports of French reconnoiters sniffing around their camp came in from Gist and other traders. Further reports said that the French mood was foul and ugly. They would surely find out about the meager numbers of British soldiers in the area. Immediate defensive action needed to be taken, and preparations were made to build a hasty fortification.

Three days later, with more reports of French activity, Lieutenant Colonel Washington sent out a scouting party of seventy-five men, which included Half King and his men. When they returned, they were eager to report that they had found a well-hidden French encampment deep in a forested gully. The camp contained a small company of no more than fifty men. Why would the French have a small hidden contingency so close by when they already had command of the fort? The possibilities filled the commander with concern, and he did not want to wait to be surprised by the answer.

With this new information, the British felt the necessity of striking first. They could easily sneak through the woods and surround the French. Washington hoped the element of surprise and having the high ground would make up for their lack of experience and numbers.

The night of May 26th was black and wet. Regardless, preparations needed to be made, and the lieutenant colonel sought Half King for a council. Fearing that an attack could occur at any time, the men agreed that they would not wait for the French to find them and make the first move—they would attack the encampment together.

At 7 a.m. the next morning, a company of forty British and a number of native allies stealthily crept through the woods as the French were stirring from their beds. One hundred yards from the French camp, they stopped. Washington sent Captain Adam Stephen and his men to the left. The native men would silently surround the far side of the camp, and Washington would take a contingent of men to the right. He knew going in that direction meant they would be exposed and in the open, and he was up for the challenge.

Modern-day Jumonville Glen.
*Rarkm_ Wikipedia_contributor, CC BY-SA 3.0 <http://creativecommons.org/licenses/by-sa/3.0/>, via Wikimedia Commons
https://commons.wikimedia.org/wiki/File:JumonvilleGlenPanorama_5_2_2007.jpg*

Once everyone was in attack position, the tall, imposing figure of Lieutenant Colonel Washington stepped out into the glen and ordered the attack. The startled French soldiers jumped up and ran for their rifles.

Shots rang out on both sides, and men began to fall.[6] The French did their best to return fire, but the readiness and high position of the British had them at a disadvantage. Bullets whistled through the air. Washington heard the sound as they passed his ears, missing his head.

The French were quickly overcome. Those who tried to run into the woods were intercepted by Half King and his contingent. After less than fifteen minutes of battle, it was over, and the French had surrendered. As many as fourteen French lay dead or wounded in the glen, among them being their commander, Joseph Coulon de Jumonville. The British had suffered only one or two wounded.

As Jumonville lay on the field, he tried to call for a ceasefire as the battle waged on. But in the heat of the fray, his call went unheeded. Now, as the smoke was clearing, he implored Washington to read the letters he clutched in his hands. If what the letters said were true, Washington had just committed the gravest error.

Before the lieutenant colonel could react to the letters, Half King walked up to the injured Jumonville. It was now his moment to enact his revenge for the humiliation at the half-built Ohio Forks outpost. As the Frenchman lay helpless and wounded, Half King allegedly said to him, "Tu n'es pas encore mort, mon père." ("Thou art not yet dead, my father.") He then took his tomahawk and crushed Jumonville's skull, killing him. He allegedly washed his hands in the

---

[6] French reports stated that the British shot first, but a British soldier involved in the conflict claimed it was difficult to know who actually took the first shot. In all likelihood, the British shot first, and the French scrambled to return the volley.

dead man's brains.[7] He had sent a clear message to the French that he was not to be trifled with.

Though short, those fifteen minutes, later dubbed the "Jumonville affair," were crucial to colonial American history.[8] In those fifteen minutes, a young, twenty-two-year-old Lieutenant Colonel George Washington had started the French and Indian War. He would not yet understand the consequences that had been set in motion.

---

[7] Accounts vary on Jumonville's death. Some accounts state that he was killed in the first volley of bullets, while other accounts tell of his death at the hands of Half King and his tomahawk. The most compelling of these is John Shaw's sworn deposition based on soldier's eyewitness accounts.

[8] Earl Horatio Walpole described the military action as "a volley fired by a young Virginian in the backwoods of America that set the world on fire."

Chapter 3 – Vengeance Visits Fort Necessity

As the British rounded up and identified prisoners, Half King and his men were feeling less charitable toward the French.[9] They plundered the dead men, and those who lay wounded were killed and scalped. In his quest for vengeance against the French, Half King also demanded that the twenty-one unwounded prisoners be turned over for the same treatment. Washington would not concede to this; he could not surrender unarmed men to be butchered, especially after he heard who they claimed to be.

Jumonville's second-in-command, Drullion, earnestly backed up Jumonville's last words and the letters he carried. He told Washington that they were emissaries on a diplomatic mission and that they had been sent to give the British a message. The letters they were bringing to the British called for their removal from the Ohio Valley.

---

[9] Only one man escaped, a French-Canadian soldier named Mouceau, who was in the woods relieving himself when the fighting broke out. He was able to report the Jumonville defeat to French commanders.

Further inspection of the letters only confirmed what the Frenchmen told them. The French claimed they wanted to keep the peace and were diplomatically demanding that the British leave their lands in the Ohio Valley under threat of forcible ejection. This mission was very similar to the one Washington himself had undertaken the year before.

Jumonville had also been under orders that if he found any British east of the Great Mountain, he was not to disturb them. But Washington and the British officers did not see this as the French trying to maintain peace. Instead, they believed these instructions painted the French contingent in the glen to be spies, sent to locate the British and scope out their numbers and positions. The British believed that the ambassadorial messages were simply a cover for the French in the event they were caught, a ruse designed to give credibility to their claims.

Furthermore, the British argued, it was quite suspicious that a supposed French ambassadorial detail would be hiding and "camping in a skulking place" deep in the glen. It was apparent that the French knew where the British were, so why would they not have already delivered the message to them? Washington wrote to Dinwiddie, giving this reasoning as a defense for his actions. He also took pains to make sure he accused the French of being the instigators.[10]

Though the Jumonville affair had been the first armed conflict of the French and Indian War, the French had previously made claims and threatened hostilities. In the minds of the British, the war had already started before the first shot was fired, and it was started by the French. Half King agreed with them on this. In his opinion, the French had always intended for hostilities to occur.[11]

---

[10] However, Washington's actions belied that claim.

[11] This book is not intended to lay the blame on either side. All sides would have their obvious biases, and their stories and opinions reflect that.

However, all of the prisoners unanimously denied the claims of the British. They continued to persist in their claims of being an embassy. Unmoved, Washington sent the French prisoners to Dinwiddie in Williamsburg. He warned the governor not to be swayed by their "many smooth stories" and that he thought "they ought to be hanged as spies of the worst sort."

Dinwiddie did not buy Washington's defense of his actions, nor his claims that the French started the affair. He knew he would have to do some damage control. In his eyes, Washington had opened fire on a camp of sleeping Frenchmen while both sides had still officially been at peace, uneasy as it was. With political suaveness, Dinwiddie told his London superiors that Half King and his men started the conflict and that Washington and his men had just backed them up. Still, Dinwiddie had a bad feeling that Earl Horatio Walpole's words were ringing true—Washington had "set the world on fire."

But Washington had bigger worries than the French prisoners or arguments over who started the conflict. When the French at Fort Duquesne heard of the essentially unprovoked attack in the glen, retribution was sure to follow. Washington believed that they would be "attacked by considerable forces" sooner rather than later. Their current camp at Great Meadows afforded no protection from an onslaught. He hadn't intended to make his stand here. Instead, he hoped to take on the French at the fortified Red Stone Creek, but he would have no choice but to make the best of it.

From the end of May to the beginning of June, the 150 men of Great Meadows tirelessly worked to build a circular fort, cutting down trees and forming them into thick stakes of seven feet high palisades covered in barks and skins. They also dug deep trenches around the outside, although the marshy ground surrounding them was thought to give the British an added advantage. When it was finished, Washington proudly bragged that when the French came against them, the fort would hold strong even if it "must withstand 5 to 1." He aptly named it Fort Necessity.

Fort Necessity today.

https://commons.wikimedia.org/wiki/File:Fort_Necessity_National_Battlefield_(b87099f5-cbd0-44ef-b776-af4e94e4787d).jpg

While the British were building the fort, Half King went on his own diplomatic mission of sorts. He carried the scalps taken from several French heads as he made his way to make a bid to persuade the Seneca, Delaware, and Shawnee warriors to join him and the British in the fight against the French.

As soon as the fort was finished, Half King showed up with about eighty Native Americans. There was not one warrior in the group. These were elderly men, women, and children seeking protection from the French. More families trickled in over the following days, but Half King's promise of warriors continued to fall flat. Not only would the British have to fight this battle on their own; now, they also had vulnerable people to protect.

That was a difficult task considering that food was running scarce. Despite writing to Alexandria, additional food provisions never came. And now Washington had native families to feed on top of his men—

and he could not give them less than he was feeding his own men. When the last sack of flour was used, the people had to endure four days of hunger before an Ohio trader came through. He sold them provisions at an exorbitant price.

Just a few days later, on June 9th, Washington saw the sight he had been waiting for—the rest of the Virginia regiment filing into the Great Meadows. The relief he felt was short-lived. These men had little battle experience and even less in the way of provisions. To top it off, the regiment's commander, Colonel Joshua Fry, was not among them. He had fallen from his horse and broke his neck, dying of his injuries. Washington would now be the senior field officer in command of the fort until the North Carolina regiment arrived. The problems they faced remained his to deal with.

Over the next few weeks, more army regulars from South Carolina made it to the fort, along with nine small swivel cannons. The sight of the small crudely built fort was enough to give the professional soldiers pause. The fort was only fifty-three feet in diameter. It contained some meager food supplies, a few tents for shelter, and numerous muddy puddles, courtesy of the weather. The soldiers did not feel confident in its protection. Instead of staying with the provincial militia inside the fort, they opted to make their own camp nearby. This was headed by their own commander, Captain James Mackay, who told Washington that he was not about to take orders from a colonial colonel. Despite the obvious snub, Washington was glad to have a force of four hundred fighting men at Fort Necessity. All the while, the French were gathering their own forces.

On June 18th, Washington had a highly disappointing meeting with Half King and the Six Nations' Council at Onondaga. Not only were they reluctant to join the fight against the French, but Half King himself was also beginning to waver on the decision. When the natives saw the British fort, it seemed like an unstable fence compared to the stronghold of Fort Duquesne. They questioned whether they wanted to ally themselves with soldiers who would barely be able to defend themselves in such a shoddy structure. The native chiefs did not like how the odds looked for the British and would not risk taking sides with an army that was sure to lose in battle. Realistically, they worried how defeat would affect their own people, fearing that a loss would bring further hostility and vengeance upon themselves should they align themselves with the British and lose.

In the end, Washington's diplomatic prowess proved embarrassingly ineffective with the native chiefs. The council, having lost trust in Washington's ability to win and fearing the superior strength of the French, decided that the Six Nations would remain neutral in the white man's fight. They took their people from the fort and left. Half King stood by Washington, and a few loyal natives joined him.

The loss of these expected native allies was a hard blow to Washington and the British. Not only was their fighting force reduced, but they were also left more vulnerable, as they now had fewer native scouts and guides. Disappointment turned to distrust. The British could not help but see the natives who refused to ally as "treacherous Devils." Some even believed they were spies for the French. Washington could not let his men see the deep concerns he had. They must press on, especially with the French numbers at Fort Duquesne growing larger and larger by the day.

Concerned with French movements, Washington ordered all of his men to clear the roads and fields in the wilderness to get back to the fort at Great Meadows. The same day he gave his order, June 28th, an avenging force of seven hundred French, Canadian, and native warriors left Fort Duquesne and headed their way.

However, the British were unaware that a smaller French force had left ahead of the main army. On July 3rd, they stood at the tree line, staring in full view of the stockade fort. The man leading the charge was none other than François Coulon de Villiers, Jumonville's older brother.

Washington's actions alone during the Jumonville affair would not have likely triggered an all-out war, insulting as the French may have found it. But the savage butchery of Jumonville and some of the others was more than the French could let slide.

When Villiers heard of his brother's death and the questionable actions that led up to it, he petitioned his commanding officer, Claude-Pierre Pécaudy de Contrecœur, to allow him to lead the retaliatory charge. He was given permission to take five hundred men and advance. Before making it to Great Meadows, he stopped at the glen where his brother had died. The bodies had been left unburied, and the summer heat created an unbearably putrid smell. Scalping and wild animals had rendered the corpses completely unrecognizable. Still, the men took the time to bury their fallen compatriots before marching on, their revenge now refreshed. They used the very road the Virginians themselves had just built.

From the tree line above, Villiers could make out the fort's stockade. He watched as the soldiers laboriously dug trenches in the viscous mud caused by the previous night's heavy rain, which had created marshy ponds around the stockade and turned the trenches into streams. This "charming field for an encounter" had been turned into a muddy, watery death trap.

As colonial sentinels looked out into the tree line, it was their turn to be surprised. Though their reconnaissance parties had brought back sensational and sometimes dubious reports of large numbers of French and native warriors, all naked, on the march to attack the British over the past week, Washington and his men were literally up to their knees in mud trying to make preparations in and around the fort. They had expected to meet the French face to face on the battlefield, but the ambush had come with unexpected swiftness.[12]

---

[12] Meeting armies face to face on the battlefield was typical in European-style battles

The sentinels grabbed their muskets and fired hastily before running back toward the fort. The French did not hesitate. The three well-disciplined columns behind Villiers advanced. They halted to fire and then continued downhill toward the trenches. The fort's soldiers positioned themselves in front of the watery trenches, ready for a full-frontal assault. Then, the French made a sudden change in direction.

Washington scrambled to position his entire force in the open field. It was a dangerous gamble, but it was the only one that could slow the French advance. But even this was just delaying the inevitable.

A chill went through the Virginia regiment as the natives gave "a great cry" and led the French charge down the hill. Mackay and his men held fast, waiting until the French were within firing range. The French were unintimidated by the British showing, and as they drew closer, shots were fired, and cannons cut down the advancing native warriors.

Washington turned to his men, only to be shocked at what he saw—none of them were there. They had fled, vaulting themselves into the watery trenches.[13] He ordered the men to fire, but their nervousness combined with battle ineptitude caused them to miss their targets. Instead, they shot too high, hitting the trees and raining down nothing more than leaves and branches upon the French.

The French, however, did not want to take any chances that those in the trenches would better their aim. The French and Native Americans dropped suddenly to the ground, concealing themselves behind any stones, stumps, trees, or bushes nearby.

To the British, it would have appeared as if their enemies had instantly vanished, except for the persistent firestorm of bullets coming toward them. But the French did not only fire upon the men. They targeted every horse, dog, and cow belonging to the fort, ensuring that they took out the enemy's transportation, canine warning system, and meat sources. Dead animal carcasses soon littered the field.

To add to their already muddy woes, "the most tremendous rain that could be conceived" began to fall. It had been hard enough keeping their gunpowder and weapons dry amidst the mire and puddles, but now it was impossible. The waterlogged, mud-laden British soon became exhausted, and the firing of their soaked flintlock weapons gradually died out. They were perplexed at how the French could possibly be keeping their own powder and weapons dry, as they seemed to have no trouble continuing to fire upon them.

At 8 p.m., the French called for a ceasefire. Raising the white flag, they shouted an invitation, "Voulez- vous parler?" It was an offer to talk. Although Washington knew they were beaten, he adamantly refused. He would not allow the French to come within the fort. Washington feared it was a ruse designed to check out their situation, which would better enable them to complete the demise of the fort and those within.

Well, Villiers told Washington via messenger, if they did not want the French to come to the fort to talk, they were more than welcome to send someone to the French camp. He was willing, perhaps with gritted teeth, to negotiate with the man whom he blamed for his brother's death. But better that than to risk colonial reinforcements arriving and the possibility of dying by the British sword.

Only two soldiers of Washington's men spoke French: Dutchman Jacob van Braam and Ensign William Le Peyronie. They were sent to the French camp for talks. Villiers did not hide the fact that his assault stemmed from the need to avenge his brother's death. However, he told the men he was feeling generous; if they vacated the fort, it would

---

[13] One soldier later wrote that Washington's second-in-command, Lieutenant Colonel George Muse, "frightened his men back to the trenches," leaving Mackay and his men vulnerable in the open.

satisfy his vengeance. Their countries were not officially at war, so he did not feel the need for further hostilities.

Peyronie and van Braam trudged back to the fort through the rain and mud, the ceasefire agreement in their hands becoming soggy and limp. The articles, with the ink runny from the rain, were translated to Washington. The British were to leave the fort, taking everything but their arsenal, and they were to do it quickly lest the French and their native allies got restless. They were also to leave behind two officers as hostages to be used in a prisoner exchange.

However, the articles also contained two interesting phrases that were not translated to Washington. Whether it was on purpose, poor translation, or the wet pages rendered unreadable by the rain, van Braam failed to say that the articles mentioned "vengor l'assassin" and "l'assasinat du Jumonville."[14] These phrases were a critical omission. The document implied that the British agreed that Jumonville was intentionally assassinated, not simply killed in battle. Signing it was as good as a confession to the crime.

The next day, July 4th, the French saw the British army out "with honors." The British banners waved in front of the departing columns, and the drums turned out a solemn beat with which to march away. The fleur-de-lis flag raised above the fort, waving above van Braam and Captain Robert Stobo, the two hostages who had been left behind.

The departing regiment had no wagons or pack animals to carry their belongings or rations, so they could only take what they could carry.[15] The French promised to guard the rest of their baggage until the British could send wagons to retrieve their things. Agreements on both sides were immediately broken.

---

[14] Neither British nor French were van Braam's first language, so there was bound to be a margin of error in translating.

[15] The French agreed under the terms of the surrender to let the British take their arms and munitions with them. Unarmed, they would have been vulnerable to attack on their march out.

As Major Adam Stephen, wet, stockingless, and muddy up to his thighs, was walking away, a servant shouted that the French were stealing his clothing. Already hot-tempered, the incensed major ran to the thief, ripped the trunk from the man's shoulders, and kicked him in the rear end. As he walked back to his line, two French soldiers stopped to chastise him, telling him if any Englishman struck one of their soldiers, they would not be responsible for the resulting retaliation. After delivering a swearing reply in which he "damned the capitulation" and pointed out the French had already been the first to break the terms, the amused Frenchmen asked if such a "dirty, half-naked" fellow could possibly be an officer. In response, he opened his trunk, pulled out a "flaming suit of laced Regimentals,"[16] and put it on over his mud and gunpowder encrusted clothes before walking away from the astonished soldiers.

However, Major Stephen was not the only one to suffer the theft of his things as they marched away. As they moved away from the fort, the natives allied with the French besieged and harassed the departing army. Having already plundered the belongings they left at the fort, they stole and mocked the exhausted soldiers. Some soldiers thought they recognized familiar faces—those of the Delaware chiefs who had only a few weeks before considered an alliance with them.[17]

Each day, the ranks of the army dwindled as deserters fled by night. Half King and the natives slipped away under cover of darkness to return to their own families and villages. Half King returned to his home in disgrace, losing the clout he had hoped to gain.[18,19] The defeat did not only reflect badly on him but also the Iroquois leadership whom he had promised a victory.

---

[16] A formal uniform.

[17] The Delaware, along with many other tribes, fell under the umbrella of Iroquois rule. They, along with other western tribes, did not want to be under the Iroquois dominion and found it advantageous to ally with the French.

[18] His home was near modern-day Harrisburg, Pennsylvania.

[19] Half King died just a few weeks later.

Washington had been seeking fame, and he quickly found it as news of Fort Necessity circulated. Only this was not the type of fame he had been looking for; he knew the defeat portrayed him in a poor light, especially after the Jumonville debacle. As with the Jumonville affair, his correspondence shows that if he thought he had made any mistakes, he wasn't admitting them. He blamed bad weather and the indifferent attitude of the soldiers for the fort's demise, never mentioning that the poorly chosen location and weak commanders under his control were the major contributing factors.

To the French, the British baggage left behind was too irresistible of a temptation. But they found more than just clothes, surveying equipment, and other mundane objects. One item caught their eye in particular—Washington's personal journal. Of course, Villiers's curiosity got the better of him, and after reading it, he forwarded it to his commanders. It eventually made it into the hands of Governor Duquesne.

Washington's innermost thoughts did nothing to endear him to the French governor, who declared that "there is nothing more unworthy and lower, even blacker than the sentiments and way of thinking of this Washington." He then wistfully stated that he wished he could have had the "pleasure to read his outrageous journal in front of his very nose." He may have missed that opportunity, but he wanted to make sure every French person knew just what a villain Washington was. So, he had the journal sent to Paris, where it was published and made available for anyone to read.

Chapter 4 – "You Should Have First Asked Our Consent"

Once back in Virginia, Washington fully expected heavy criticism and blame for the loss of the fort. Although he received a mild rebuke from Dinwiddie, he was even more surprised when the House of Burgesses passed a vote thanking him and the other officers. Some of them personally approached him. If Washington basked in their thanks and condolences on his defeat, it didn't last long.

Dinwiddie wanted to send a regiment back to Ohio as soon as possible. But he was without the manpower, so he was stuck waiting for British reinforcements. In the meantime, sick of squabbling between colonials and regulars, he decided to reorganize the Virginia regiment into smaller units headed by captains. Dinwiddie offered Washington a captaincy with the regular army. Apparently forgetting the fiascos he was recently the cause of, Washington was offended by the offer of a lower rank than the one he currently held. He told Dinwiddie that there was no way he could be satisfied with a lower rank than he deserved or "thought he had the right to." He resigned from the army and went back to tending his farm.

Though the story of Washington's involvement at the beginning of the conflict was crucial to the events that followed, it was not the only story. Those first conflicts touched off an intricate web of other conflicts, allies, enemies, and trading partners that was spun throughout the colonial empire. Alliances, particularly with the indigenous tribes, were of the utmost importance. But negotiations, diplomacy, and maintaining good relationships proved tricky for some.

Various colonies took advantage of the decentralized system that imbued local governments with a lot of power.[20] They took it upon themselves to form their own relationships with the tribes of the Six Nations. The alliances in themselves were not a problem, but the fact that each colony was invested only in their own interests and made deals without concern for the well-being of any other colonies or those with whom they were allying themselves proved problematic. This became a real concern to British leadership overseeing the individual colonies. If alliances with the natives were not carefully managed, it would be harmful to the British cause.

The greatest and probably most disastrously chaotic example of this problem happened at a meeting in Albany, which had been called by the newly appointed governor Sir Danvers Osborn. The New England states, Virginia,[21] Maryland, and Pennsylvania[22] were called to meet with the Iroquois confederation.[23] Osborn, however, would never make it to the meeting. Tragically, two days after his arrival in

---

[20] Some historians believe that local governments were allowed too much power. As a result, conflicts over trade and land were common.

[21] Dinwiddie refused to send a representative despite the invitation.

[22] Pennsylvania was reluctant to send a representative at first. Benjamin Franklin was eventually sent to join the meeting.

[23] Prior to this meeting, the Iroquois council had a meeting amongst themselves. They saw "the storm clouds of war" on the horizon and needed a strategy. But it seemed like a lose-lose situation. Though this was a "white man's war," fighting for one side or another would likely mean fighting against other native tribes who allied themselves with the opposite side. But if they remained neutral, they were likely to be just sitting idly by as their land was stolen by the warring powers.

New York City, he was dead, a victim of suicide by his own handkerchief. This left a heavy-handed Lieutenant Governor James DeLancey in charge, a man who let the power he had just gained go to his head.

After the delegates took their seats in Albany, five weeks of bickering commenced. The delegates knew that everyone was serving their own interests, so deep distrust had infected them before the talks even began.

New Yorkers, who were backed by DeLancey, considered the Iroquois "their" allies and were aggravated by any other colony trying to "interfere" with what they had going on. Using the authority of his gavel, DeLancey maintained strict control of the floor, claiming it was his right of superiority, considering he was the only governor present. Delegates objected to his handling of the talks, but he would not allow anything to be discussed that might cast New York in a bad light or conflict with its interests. This served to stifle discussions that might bring about solutions to problems like corruption.

On July 2nd, DeLancey began to discuss the French threat and the importance of native allies in helping to neutralize it. After weeks of colonists squabbling over who had the right to ally with native nations, it was finally time to hear from the Iroquois delegations. King Hendrick, a Mohawk leader, took the floor. What he said was meant as a knock on the heads of colonial representatives, calling them to their senses.

After noting the governor's opening comments, Hendrick took the stick in his hand and threw it behind his back. The dramatic move certainly caught the attention of the delegates, and they listened to his next words. Directing himself to DeLancey, Hendrick revealed the meaning of the stick. "You have thus thrown us behind your back and discarded us."

The Iroquois felt that the British had taken their good relationship and alliance for granted, and it did not go unnoticed. One of the biggest complaints was against the Albany colonists. Due to their proximity and other factors, they had a monopoly on the fur trade with the indigenous tribes. Knowing that, the colonists slyly offered to pay low prices, knowing there was no one else to offer more. As a result, the native tribes did not get much money to buy trade goods, so the trading became unfair and one-sided.

But as the British colonies made alliances based on their own interests with little regard for the people they made them with, the French took a different approach—and it worked very well. Hendrick pointed this out, "The French are...ever using their utmost endeavors to seduce and bring our people over to them."

However, the biggest issue the Iroquois had with this situation was their lands. They were being fought over and taken without even consulting the people who had the rights to them, not to mention the long-term consequences it would have on the natives. Hendrick's sentiments echoed those of Tanacharison's, as he had believed that the land given to his people came from a divine source. But now the French and British were coming in on either side of the river to divide it up. Where would it leave his people?

The Mohawk king did not mince words when he said directly, "The governor of Virginia and the governor of Canada are both quarreling about lands that belong to us, and such a quarrel as this may end in our destruction." He further added a condemnation of their actions. "[The governors] have made paths through our country to trade and build houses without acquainting us with it. They should have first asked our consent."

With a scathing denunciation of their strategies, he concluded his speech, saying, "Look at the French, they are men, they are fortifying everywhere. But we are ashamed to say it, you are all like women, bare and open without any fortifications."

If King Hendrick had meant to shame the colonists into taking more honorable actions, it did not work. His forthright speech fell on deaf ears. The delegates kept their focus on their interests—taking more land. The motives may have varied. Some wanted land for profit,[24] others had political motivations, and others had more grandiose notions of a national council over local and native affairs. The delegates promised to consider the native council's complaints and demands, but they had little power or motivation to actually do anything about them.

However, the delegates were unwisely ignoring the fundamental issues that Hendrick had pointed out—not only the taking of land and resources without the consent of the natives who owned the land but also the lack of any reciprocation, which is the very foundation of an alliance.[25] The only reason more tribes hadn't taken sides with the French was out of fear of British military power. It was also pointed out to them that if they wanted to battle the French for the lands, they were way behind their rivals. They were failing to take the most basic necessary actions to even hold the lands they were claiming.

The colonial delegates seemed to think these issues were of almost no consequence. It couldn't be further from the truth. George Washington himself insightfully pointed out the importance of maintaining good relationships and native alliances, noting, "Indians are the only match for Indians, and without them [on our side] we shall ever fight on unequal terms." The French knew this important truth as well, even if Washington's comrades did not see it. And it was that willful ignorance that would come back to haunt them.

---

[24] Some delegates plied the natives with liquor until they agreed to sell their land.

[25] This was more than just the taking of the land; it was about broken promises made to the native people just a few years earlier. In 1752, Half King negotiated on behalf of the Iroquois nations. He was told that the Virginians wanted to *buy* the land from them so that they could resell it to the settlers. These would be "bought" by trading with cheap goods. A colonial spokesman further tried to reassure the tribes, promising, "Brethren, be assured that the King...by purchasing your lands, had never any intention of taking them from you, but that we might live together as one people, and keep them from the French, who would be bad neighbors." Ironically, it was now they who were being condemned by the indigenous people as "bad neighbors."

Chapter 5 – Wilderness War

As the colonies bickered amongst themselves, the clamor was but a mere buzz over in London. But despite the political wrangling going on amidst the British aristocracy, everyone agreed on one thing—the French needed to be expelled from "their" North American territories. This means more troops needed to be sent to Virginia. That is, *almost* everyone agreed with this. Secretary of State Thomas Pelham-Holles, Duke of Newcastle, believed that the French threat was being overly exaggerated. He believed that, overall, the French were peaceable, and diplomacy over force was the answer. King George II agreed with him. After six years of official peace with France, he was reluctant to set off another war.[26] He and Newcastle held a "let Americans fight Americans" attitude and refused to send more British soldiers.

But after several months of pressure and prodding, Newcastle finally caved. It was obvious that the colonial militia alone was not up to the challenge. Two regiments of Irish Redcoats under the

---

[26] Despite the armed conflicts occurring in North America, no official declaration of war had been made.

command of Major General Edward Braddock were told to set sail across the Atlantic.

Though Braddock was well-connected, the major general had far too little experience on the front lines. His strengths lay in logistics and administration, but the London leadership felt he was the most obvious choice to help halt the growing crisis in America.[27]

Braddock was about to experience wilderness warfare in a baptism of fire. He was given four specific assignments—get the French out of Ohio,[28] take the New York forts at Niagara and Crown Point from the French, and then destroy Fort Beauséjour in Nova Scotia.

It was to be a ridiculously daring and difficult three-pronged simultaneous attack. That tour covered a dauntingly long distance through the harsh and unforgiving mountain wilderness. Braddock would have his work cut out for him.

He left in late December 1754, and the winter trip across the ocean was risky. But as stormy and miserable as the six-week journey was, Braddock was determined to beat the French across the ocean. He had the advantage over the French preparations, as he was able to land on the more moderately temperate Virginia shores even though it was winter. The French, however, were locked out of continental Canada by ice-enclosed ports and would not be able to disembark until sometime in the spring. That gave Braddock several months to prepare.

Braddock would desperately need that time too. Though his regiments looked good on paper, the Irish units were relatively weak. However, Braddock was under the impression that the backwoods forces of the French, Canadian, and tribal fighters would be no match for his army regulars. Still, his forces would need the colonial numbers, especially with such ambitious assignments ahead of him.

---

[27] Braddock had also held the post of governor of Gibraltar.
[28] This would be accomplished by capturing Fort Duquesne, near present-day Pittsburgh, Pennsylvania.

Putting together a worthy army would prove harder than Braddock thought. He wondered what the colonists had been doing all this time. There were no weapon stockpiles, no major numbers of new recruits, and those who had been recruited were not properly trained and disciplined. Braddock also faced the logistical nightmare of getting men and supplies over the mountains into Ohio.

By spring, Braddock had two thousand British regular soldiers, nine hundred colonial militiamen, and fifty native warriors ready for battle. A detailed map of Fort Duquesne, which had been drawn by a British officer imprisoned as a war hostage, was intercepted in an attempt to smuggle it to Williamsburg. It proved to be a highly valuable capture. The British found out that Fort Duquesne now only had four hundred men garrisoned within its walls rather than the one thousand plus previously reported. Braddock was confident that he had the statistical advantage over the fort. The biggest problem he would face was getting there.

He and his men would have to march over one hundred miles, crossing the Allegheny Mountains on the way. It would be a challenge for a leader not accustomed to the wilderness and a large army carrying supplies. He would need an aide—someone familiar with those mountains and forests. The man he needed was George Washington.

Braddock didn't know it yet, but he also sorely needed Washington to bridge the gap between his royalist sensibilities and the rugged provincials living off the land. Braddock threw the full weight of his royally commissioned position around, and the more he did, the more his demands angered the locals, who were already looking to live a life free from the royalist yolk. They cared nothing about the empires that fought over the land and were not sympathetic to the cause.

Braddock soon realized he was facing an issue he was wholly unaccustomed to—nobody in the colonies, not even the governors, felt compelled to follow orders. They bickered, made promises they never intended to keep, and regularly indulged themselves in petty jealousies. It was a far cry from the strict army discipline and obedience to orders he expected.

Despite Braddock's political ineptitude and lack of military experience, the governors agreed to a preposterous plan that would bring nothing but utter disaster. It was decreed that Braddock's four missions would be conducted *simultaneously* despite the great distances between the forts they were tasked to seize.[29] But this way, Braddock could metaphorically kill four birds with one stone, and the governors benefited from supply contracts, prestigious military commands, and receiving favor from British authority. The overreaching ambition of Braddock and the governors would be their doom.

---

[29] Each task commander would face their own immense challenge. Braddock took on the key operation of Fort Duquesne, a crucial location on the Ohio Forks that basically guarded the entire Ohio Country. Next, the highly inexperienced Massachusetts governor William Shirley was assigned to take his two American militia regiments the three hundred miles from Albany to Fort Niagara, crossing difficult terrain that included slow, arduous ship portages and traversing a lake. Once there, he would come against a formidable French force sitting among the easy protection of Lake Ontario and the St. Lawrence River. Colonel William Johnson was assigned Fort Saint-Frédéric, an imposing, well-manned fortress at Crown Point that would require the help of the Iroquois to conquer. Nova Scotia Lieutenant Governor Charles Lawrence was assigned to take on Fort Beauséjour. Although the fort itself was weak from disrepair and had few soldiers holding it, the Acadians and Micmac natives who lurked there played by their own rules. They used the crumbling walls to their advantage and held it as a point from which they could conduct guerilla warfare.

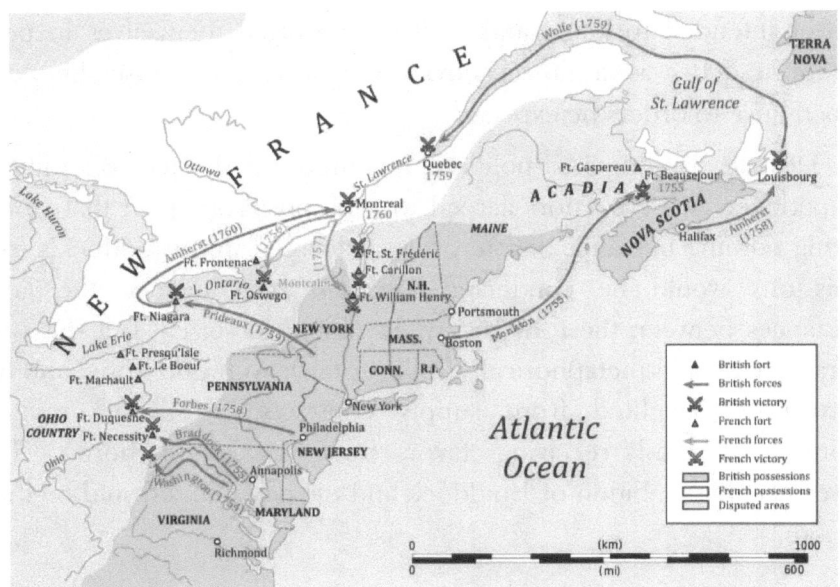

Map of British campaigns against French forts.

Hoodinski, CC BY-SA 3.0 <https://creativecommons.org/licenses/by-sa/3.0>, via Wikimedia Commons https://commons.wikimedia.org/wiki/File:French_and_indian_war_map.svg

Besides being too ambitious in his campaigns, Braddock made another fatal error in judgment. When the native chiefs offered men to help him conquer Fort Duquesne, he brashly refused. Despite Washington's solid belief in the necessity of indigenous allies, Braddock's arrogance told him differently. He believed that European battle tactics were far superior to anything the indigenous warriors and scouts could offer, even telling Benjamin Franklin that "Duquesne can hardly detain me three or four days."

He not only declined the help but also heaped further insult upon the chiefs. He bluntly told them that the army would not allow their people to remain in the Ohio Valley once the British won the war. Soured, the chiefs told him that "if they might not have liberty to live on the land," they would refuse to fight for it. Then the native men who did not return to their villages traveled to where they might be better appreciated—Fort Duquesne.

With George Washington by his side as a volunteer aide and Benjamin Franklin's deft negotiations to secure wagons from local farmers, Braddock set off for Fort Cumberland, which was one hundred miles from Fort Duquesne. The men began their trek on a hopeful note, but the reality of traveling through dense, virgin woods and difficult, rocky, mountainous terrain soon crashed down on them. Even where they built rudimentary "roads," the pack horses were hardly able to travel the muddy, tree rooted, and boulder-strewn paths, never mind wagons carrying howitzers and other artillery and supplies.[30] Progress was painstakingly slow. Some days the caravan only made it seven miles over the course of eight hours. The trek took over two months.

When they reached the crudely built Fort Cumberland on Saturday, May 10th, 1755, it was not much to look at. The men set up camp. To their surprise, no locals came to sell them fresh food. Assuming the men were intercepting the locals and buying it on the sly, Braddock threatened death to any man caught doing so. He had not yet realized that they were very alone in the wilderness. There *were* no locals. The supplies they brought were all they had.

Still, the arrival of the troops to the fort created an atmosphere of a bustling, if not rowdy, town. Though Braddock tried to keep the troops occupied with drills and training, they often found better uses of their time, at least in their eyes.[31] Natives led by Tanacharison's successor, Scarouady, came into the camp and helped stir things up. They amused and impressed the soldiers with wild stories of their adventures and performed native war dances. However, it all became too much for Braddock when he found out that the native women were coming in and "entertaining" the troops for money and that soldiers were freely sharing liquor with their new indigenous friends.

---

[30] Once they began their inland march, there was nowhere to resupply for miles, so they had to bring what they could.

[31] Almost a third of his men were militiamen—nonprofessional soldiers recruited into the army. They had little to no training as opposed to the army regulars who were professional, trained soldiers.

Fort Cumberland, 1755.

https://commons.wikimedia.org/wiki/File:Fort_cumberland.jpg

Widespread drunkenness, bad behavior, and the lack of even the most basic military discipline among the men were huge problems for Braddock. He ordered harsh punishments for anyone found carousing with women, sharing liquor, or being otherwise disorderly—anywhere from garnishment of wages to 250 lashes to a death sentence. It was a look into how the imperial army was run, and many of the colonists did not like what they saw.

They were not the only ones. Disgusted by what they felt was Braddock's "bad heart," heavy-handed tactics, and general scorn for them, the majority of the fifty native men who enlisted to help the British left. Only eight stayed, including a now sullen Scarouady and his son. Again, the allies they sorely needed were driven away.

Braddock turned his attention back to his mission. Although he had absolutely no concrete knowledge of what was happening at Fort Duquesne, his arrogant nature once again assumed that the enemy there was weak and nearly defenseless.[32] He believed the moment they

---

[32] This was mainly due to his lack of native scouts. He told his superiors in London that he doubted he could rely on them for accurate information anyway.

saw his mighty army march up, they would abandon their post and run northward.

But not long after they left Fort Cumberland, native scouts began to report that French reinforcements were on their way to Fort Duquesne. Braddock cursed their slow movements and likely cursed Benjamin Franklin's erroneous prediction that the trip would be "light and easy."

After three days of agonizingly slow progress, Braddock decided to send the heaviest wagons back. The problem was, they contained the howitzers and a large chunk of their powder and munitions—supplies that were exactly essential in a battle.

Washington told Braddock that there was no way he was going to be able to capture the fort since they were bogged down by their snail-like pace. He suggested that they break up their forces and send a smaller contingent to ride ahead of the main column. Braddock liked the idea, but it was one that would prove to be disastrous.

On June 18th, Braddock set out with about half his army and as many munitions as they could quickly haul. However, he would leave the rest of the men to follow with too few wagons and horses, and they quickly fell behind. Even unburdened with half his army and supplies, Braddock's progress was still too slow. He now had two choices, and neither of them was great. He either could continue on at the same pace and risk French reinforcements beating him to Fort Duquesne or ditch more of his artillery and munitions but face the possibility of a siege he was unprepared to win. His caution won out, much to the exasperation of Washington.[33]

On June 23rd, scouts came back to the camp to deliver good and bad news to Braddock. The bad news was that the reinforcements had reached Fort Duquesne. But the good news was that they were

---

[33] Because they were traveling through the wilderness, men had to go ahead of the wagons to cut trees and clear paths to build crude roads that made the way passable, making for a slow and difficult passage.

desperately low on food and supplies, making a long siege untenable for those inside.

However, unbeknownst to Braddock, the French were fully aware of his mission and had been almost from the beginning. French spies knew what he was going to do almost the moment he opened his commission letter. Accordingly, the French put their highly skilled Canadian Marines and local woodsmen militia into action to prepare and wait for Braddock to show up. They were also aware of Braddock's slow pace and aimed to take advantage of it. Stealthy French soldiers and their equally ghost-like native allies went out from the fort on a mission to terrorize the already unnerved British and colonial soldiers. Though Braddock's men increasingly saw evidence of the enemy in the woods around their encampment, the enemies themselves remained unseen.

Whether this rendered Braddock's men complacent to the danger or just reckless, three soldiers wandered from Braddock's camp one evening. Suddenly, the sound of musket fire crashed through the June air. Men ran from the camp in search of their compatriots, fearing what had caused them to fire. It did not take long for them to find out. The three bodies of the missing soldiers lay in the dirt, their scalps having been removed from their heads. Braddock was angered, and hunting parties went out. But fear of their ferocious and nearly invisible enemy got the better of them. Every creak of the branch and rustle of the leaves set their trigger fingers in motion, and the men fired about wildly and without discipline. But there was no one there to receive their shots.

Only three soldiers may have died, but the action was highly effective in throwing Braddock's men off-balance. The French were not done with them, but they had bought themselves some much-needed time.

In truth, Duquesne commander Claude-Pierre Pécaudy de Contrecœur was worried about how well the fort walls would be able to hold up to the British cannons. He knew his best chance at victory was meeting the British outside of the fort walls, and he set his men to clearing fields on which they could "greet" the British army. While some worked on clearing the area, Contrecœur had soldiers and natives form raiding parties to help break the British advance as well as their morale.

With the bulk of the Troupes de Marine scattered about French Canada in small detachments, it would take time to get them to Fort Duquesne. Fortunately, some surprising yet welcomed allies showed up at their gates. The Ohio natives were offended by Braddock, and they were now eager to make amends with the French, especially since it appeared they had the superior fighting skills. They begged the French to forgive them for choosing to take sides with the British. They realized their mistake and wanted to pledge loyalty to and fight for the French.

The French now had many native allies, but Contrecœur proved to be a problem. Besides the poor state of the fort, his age was catching up to him. On top of this, he did not have enough men to comfortably take on the much larger British force. He called north for reinforcements. At the end of June, Contrecœur had a moment of relief when he saw the canoes of French Captain Daniel Hyacinthe Liénard de Beaujeu coming to the riverbank. Relief quickly turned to alarmed disappointment when he saw that only two hundred men had come with Beaujeu, which was far fewer men than anticipated or needed. There were also no additional weapons.

After conferring on the state of the fort and the number of men there to defend it, both men agreed that the fort was a lost cause. There was no way they could hold it when the British showed up—they didn't have the manpower or the weapons. They felt that the best course would be to do what the British anticipated they would—retreat north to the safety of the much larger and more important Fort Niagara.

However, Beaujeu came up with an idea. Maybe, just maybe, a small contingent could stay and deal the British a quick blow by using the element of surprise. They would send out raiding parties to ambush and harass Braddock's men. There were no fantasies of winning against the British; this was just a plan to buy time so that the bulk of the garrison could escape north. But Beaujeu would need to get the help of their native allies.

Beaujeu had been friendly with the local tribes for many years, so he was well-acquainted enough with their ways to know that they would never want to make a last stand in a doomed French fort. But perhaps they would help with their delay tactics.

He met with a council of twelve nations from the colonies and Canada, which included the Abenaki, Shawnee, Delaware, and members of the Six Nations. When Beaujeu told them he wanted help against the British, they scoffed and told him that he had "no sense." Even with the natives, the French would be outnumbered, and they were unwilling to sacrifice themselves for a cause that was not even their own. Still, they told him they would sleep on it and give an official decision the next day.

On the day he was to head out, Beaujeu first stopped and asked the chaplain for his blessing. As he left the chapel, dressed in native war clothes and painted skin,[34] the native chiefs were waiting for him with their decision. They would not fight. While Beaujeu pleaded with them, a native scout ran into the camp. The British army was close; they had already crossed the Monongahela River. Beaujeu made one last pleading speech. Whether he felt emboldened or put on a façade for the natives, he told them, "You see my friends, the British are going to throw themselves into the lion's mouths. They are weak sheep who pretend to be ravenous wolves." He told them all they needed to do was wait in hiding until he and his men made their move, and then they could come out and back them up in battle. He

---

[34] This was done as a symbol of friendship and solidarity.

confidently told them, "The victory is ours!" His speech worked. He was greeted with war whoops in response, and 650 native warriors were now ready to fight with him.

Unlike the British, who were loudly and methodically marching with drums and fifes signaling their every move, the French and Native American forces stealthily ran undetected through the forest toward the advancing army. The British engineers, who were at the front of the column, continued their work of cutting and clearing the way, making it possible to drive the wagons through.

So, wholly unaware of the French and native presence, the morale among the British and colonists was high. Braddock believed that by the evening, they would be drinking champagne and celebrating their victory behind the walls of Fort Duquesne, which was now only seven miles away.

Their high spirits changed to fear at the speed of light. It seemed as if Beaujeu and his horde instantaneously appeared, crashing out of the brush and landing in front of them, whooping and firing scattered shots. As a British horseman called back that a native attack was upon them, Beaujeu and his men disappeared back into the dense woods as quickly as they had come out.

Although Braddock and his officers had expected the French to meet them in battle along the way to Fort Duquesne, this had caught them by surprise. The British quickly fell into ranks and dropped to one knee, beginning their volleys. One rank would shoot and then fall back for the next to take their shots, reloading as fast as they could. They shot blindly into the woods, the smoke created from the volleys further blinding them to the enemy's whereabouts. Panic began to take hold.

Yet, unbeknownst to the British forces, a shot from their third volley hit its mark. Beaujeu lay dead on the forest floor with the fatal musket ball still in his head. Captain Jean-Daniel Dumas was now in command of the French effort.

Still under cover of dense foliage, the Canadian and native warriors swiftly moved to flank the British grenadiers, who were distracted by the formation of French regulars who came out to meet them face to face on the road. From their invisible perches, they carefully aimed and sniped each of the grenadiers one by one. Whereas the British were firing blindly at the invisible snipers in the woods, French eyes carefully marked their easy targets since they wore red coats and clumped together. Within minutes, the majority of General Thomas Gage's officers lay dead or wounded. Though some brave soldiers stayed and fought fiercely after the death of their commanders, most broke rank and scattered.

Braddock tried to bring the remaining eight hundred men and their munitions forward. But the road was in no condition to support a quick advance of this kind. With the first flanks now running back toward them, the situation descended into chaos. The confusion allowed the French and Native Americans to get to higher ground, allowing them to have the advantage. They fired shot after shot into the reeling British ranks.

Washington had knowledge of the guerilla-style warfare the French and natives were now bringing down upon them, and he begged Braddock to let him take his Virginia regiment into the woods to do the same. Stubbornly, Braddock refused to allow any of his men to deviate from the traditional battle formations.

As Braddock was trying to bring things back under control and shouting orders at his men, his voice suddenly fell silent. The next moment, he slid from his horse's saddle and fell to the ground, struck by enemy fire. However, the aging Braddock survived and mounted another horse. He persevered in battle as, one by one, his horses were shot out from under him. Four of his horses fell that day.

Braddock's officers did not fare as well as he did. The French, who especially targeted the commanders, shot until all were dead or wounded. By mid-afternoon, Braddock saw that their situation was dire. Almost half of his men were down, either dead, dying, or wounded. He had to order a retreat. The men did not have to be told twice.

While retreating, Braddock suddenly felt the hot tear of his flesh as a shot ripped straight through his arm and into his side. He fell from his fifth horse, mortally wounded. The British abandoned everything and everyone as the French and natives chased them back across the river. They continued to slaughter or capture anyone they could reach. The small river ran red with blood.

The British retreated back to their wagon train. Seeing the state of their compatriots as they fled back, the wagon drivers began to panic. They cut the horses loose and rode away, leaving their wagons behind.

George Washington, who was unhurt but horrified, later said that what he saw that day was nearly "indescribable" in its nature and that the sounds of the dead and dying were enough to "pierce the heart" of even the most stoic warrior. But Washington was also disgusted by what he felt was cowardice on the part of the enlisted militiamen who were the first to turn and run. However, he desperately needed their help in getting the gravely injured Braddock to safety. Washington and another officer promised money to any who would assist them in moving their dying general. They were finally able to put Braddock in a cart and get him back across the river.

In the days after, those who had not deserted made it back to Great Meadows. Braddock was also brought there, arriving on July 13th, the same day he died from his wounds. General Thomas Dunbar, whose men were in poor shape, then took the remainder of the army back to Fort Cumberland.[35]

Washington decried the execution of Braddock's operation as "folly." He knew that the French would likely try to meet them in the woods outside the fort, but Braddock's overconfidence and

---

[35] Fifty-four women had also gone on Braddock's march, working as cooks and laundresses for the soldiers. Only four returned with the defeated army. Though some died, likely by the hands of indigenous warriors, many were kidnapped and taken to Canada to be ransomed by the French.

inflexibility kept the men from being prepared and fighting in a style that matched that of the enemy.

Meanwhile, back at Fort Duquesne, the French and native warriors were celebrating. They were not interested in pursuing the British across the river to finish them off, which was what the European soldiers would have done, but the native allies of the French returned to the battlefield to collect their spoils.[36] The warriors scalped and stripped every dead and wounded British soldier left on the ground while the French collected all the wagons, weapons, and munitions the British left behind.[37,38] It was quite a surprise windfall, especially given that they were not expecting this sort of outcome.

But the biggest prize came in a small box. Someone had found Braddock's dispatch box, and it contained the best surprise of all—information. The French now had all of Braddock's secret war plans in their hands, including instructions for the four big missions and a planned attack on Fort Oswego in western New York. The dispatches were immediately sent to Quebec. The British may have had the superior numbers, but the French now had the upper hand.

---

[36] The native warriors had not joined the fight for power or supremacy; they were satisfied in their victory of driving the British from their land.

[37] The British and colonial forces lost nearly one thousand men, while the French and native contingent lost only twenty-one men.

[38] James Smith, a British soldier being held captive at Fort Duquesne, quietly awaited the British victory, fully expecting to see his own army come to claim the fort and rescue him. Instead, he saw the French and native warriors return on the road with about a dozen captives. He was horrified to see one man tied to a stake and burned, which was somewhat common in the native tradition of torturing captives. He was later adopted into a Native American family and lived with them for six years.

Chapter 6 – Canadian Campaigns Bring British Victory

As Braddock marched toward disaster, Lieutenant Colonel Robert Monckton was headed toward the first and only British victory of the year. His aim was the seizure of Fort Beauséjour, which was strategically located on the Isthmus of Chignecto.[39] Though it was small, it was important for French movements between Quebec and Nova Scotia,[40] and the British were keen on disrupting this key advantage.

Monckton and 2,400 men left their base at Fort Lawrence on June 4th, 1755. Monckton was aware of his superior numbers, believing that there were one thousand men at the fort. But he had heard rumors that the Acadians and Micmac natives who lurked around the fort played by their own rules. They used the fort as a strategic location from which they could conduct guerilla warfare, making the situation unpredictable for the British.

---

[39] Located in Nova Scotia.
[40] Part of a region known as Acadia at the time

Fort Beauséjour's commander, Louis Du Pont Duchambon de Vergor, was well aware that the British were on their way. However, this was little comfort to him. He knew the crumbling fort walls were weakened by disrepair, and they were absurdly outnumbered—only 165 men held the fort. Even after coercing the local Acadians to help him come hold the fort, there were only four hundred French, Acadians, and native warriors.[41] Fear began to rise. Vergor knew that their only chance for survival lay in shoring up their defenses.

He set Louis-Thomas Jacau de Fiedmont to lead the men in strengthening defenses around the fort as well as burning bridges and destroying roads to slow the British advance. Meanwhile, Vergor wrote desperate letters to nearby Fort Gaspareaux, as well as Quebec and other Canadian forts and settlements, begging for reinforcements that would never come.

---

[41] The Acadians, who were French Catholics, were resistant to a takeover by the British Protestant forces, fearing religious intolerance. They were reluctant to help Vergor, afraid that if they fought on the French side and lost, they would face the possibility of execution by the British. So, they made Vergor "force" them to fight so that if they were captured by the British, they could claim that the French commander had given them no choice.

Fort Beauséjour
Verne Equinox, CC BY-SA 3.0 <http://creativecommons.org/licenses/by-sa/3.0/>, via Wikimedia Commons https://commons.wikimedia.org/wiki/File:Beausejour2006.jpg

As the British rebuilt the bridge Fiedmont had destroyed and crossed the Missaguash River, minor skirmishes with French patrols erupted. The first of these was very telling. On June 4th, French forces faced off against the British in battle formation, but things quickly fell apart and ended in a retreat. The incident only served to strengthen British confidence while exposing the French forces' weaknesses and causing their morale to tumble. It was blatantly obvious that the Acadian militia was weak and inexperienced in battle. A deeper problem than training was also glaringly exposed—the Acadians' fear and lack of motivation to fight was going to be an issue on the day of battle.

Vergor's desperation was also out in the open. Seeing the weakness of his offensive earlier that day, further defensive action seemed to be his only choice. That same night, he took drastic action, burning homes, shops, and other buildings around the fort. As the Acadians saw their residences and livelihoods going up in flames, morale further plummeted, along with their motivation to fight or work on defenses.

Skirmishes continued over the next few days, but on June 8th, the native allies brought an unexpected "guest" to the fort. They had captured a British officer. Vergor and the French officers pressed him for information, but what they heard caused their hearts to drop. The British officer was all too glad to let them know that the British were on their way with a large force, and it was backed up by heavy artillery. That heavy artillery was sure to be the end of the fort.

As small skirmishes continued to be lost in the succeeding days, the situation continued to darken for the French. When British artillery began to shake the enfeebled walls of the fort, the full weight of how badly they were outmatched fell on Vergor. The Acadians saw it clearly as well, and many began to desert the fort. Vergor's only hope was that the letters he sent out would see results and that reinforcements would show up at any moment.

That last hope was dashed on June 14th. The worst news Vergor could hear reached the fort—the British were blocking the port at Louisburg, and French reinforcements could not make it. No help was coming. Vergor could not bring himself to tell his men, fearing it would break their already weakened spirits. Still, word got out, and once it did, the men of the fort became hopeless. Those who didn't desert right then and there pushed Vergor to surrender. But Vergor was not ready to give up the fight, even if his men were.[42]

The British continued their artillery assault without letting up. The final straw came on June 16th when mortar fire hit the fort's mess hall, killing several French officers and their British prisoner. This was the end. The white flag of surrender was raised, and the terms of

---

[42] Eighty men deserted at the news of the blockade.

surrender were drawn up.⁴³ The same day, the British flag was raised over the fort.

Emboldened, Monckton next set his sights on nearby Fort Gaspareaux. He offered them the same terms he offered Vergor, and they were immediately accepted. However, when Monckton turned toward Fort Menagoueche in New Brunswick, French Marines commander Charles Boishébert refused the terms. He was not about to hand his fort over to the British. Instead, he burned it down and took his men up the river into the wilderness, where they could better position themselves for guerilla warfare.

Though the British claimed victory over a small number of French forces in Canada, the battle was a pivotal point in the history of North America and Europe. It not only changed the fate of the Acadians but also reshaped Atlantic Canada. It was also the opening British offensive victory in the Seven Years' War, an epic struggle for supremacy between the British and French empires.⁴⁴

However, farther south, more dramatic but less successful events were unfolding for the British.

---

⁴³ In the terms, Vergor insisted that protections for the Acadians be included. Though the British spared their lives, the Acadians were driven from their home. Many were taken south to Fort Edward, a British garrison in New York. Eventually, the Acadians were driven farther south, all the way down to French-held Louisiana. Today, the descendants of those Acadians are known as Cajuns (the French word Acadian was, over time, shortened to Cadian, which later morphed into Cajun).

⁴⁴ The Seven Years' War, a conflict that stemmed from European succession arguments, took place mainly in the European arena, though it is generally considered to be the first global conflict in history. However, as the war ran concurrently with the French and Indian War (1754-1763), tensions between the British and French empires spilled over into the North American colonies. In the end, it would have a dramatic effect on French occupancy and power in Europe and North America.

Chapter 7 – The "Bloody" Battles Set the Stage in New York

As the British were gaining victory in their goals in Canada, taking over the New York forts was not going as well. Governor William Shirley began his trek to Fort Oswego, which he would use as a base to launch an attack on Fort Niagara across Lake Ontario. Shirley was another inexperienced commander, and he was unaware of just how daunting a mountainous wilderness march would be, especially with winter weather looming. Thus, Shirley underestimated the difficulty of bringing his two regiments from Albany to Oswego.

Wrapped in a logistical nightmare, Shirley was forced to give up after a few weeks. He knew he would not be able to reach the fort before the cold weather set in, and continuing the trip through the harsh Adirondack winter would be equivalent to a slow, painful death. He was forced to abandon his plans and return to Albany. However, he didn't want this prong of Braddock's plan to sit in hibernation all winter. He knew that even if he had made it to Oswego, the fort was in such poor shape that it could not be defended against a French assault. So, he sent seven hundred unfortunate men to the fort to make repairs over the winter in the hopes that the plan could be revisited once the ice melted.

Farther south, as Braddock was fighting for the Ohio Forks in the summer of 1755, Irish General William Johnson was on his mission to take over the Lake Champlain/Lake George region.[45] Like Braddock, he was wealthy and well-connected, but since he was a merchant, he had little experience on the battlefield. However, unlike Braddock, Johnson had some very important qualifications to bring to the battlefield—he had an intimate knowledge of native culture and politics. With those qualifications came an important friend: Mohawk Chief Hendrick. Johnson was diametrically opposed to Braddock's contemptuous outlook on the native people. He had embraced their culture, and it would make a world of difference for the British.[46]

Even though he had about 1,500 colonial militiamen for his campaign, no native allies had signed up to accompany him. This presented a real problem, as it would leave him at a great disadvantage, especially since the French would have native allies fighting with them. But given the recent record of the British army, along with the shadow of the Albany tensions still looming over them, how could he make such an offer sound appealing?

Besides the Iroquois Confederacy's general policy of remaining neutral in the fighting, the Mohawks were a divided nation.[47] This not only posed a problem for them—many New York Mohawks were reluctant to fight their Canadian brethren allied with the French—but it was a problem for the British and French who each mistrusted their Mohawk allies, thinking they wouldn't help their cousins. But Johnson knew he had to put his suspicions aside.

---

[45] At the time, it was known by its French name: Lac du Saint Sacrement. It was renamed Lake George by Johnson in honor of the British king.
[46] The Mohawk nicknamed Johnson "Chief Big Business."
[47] The Mohawk tribe is part of the more encompassing Iroquois Confederacy.

Johnson, who became the newly named British liaison to the Iroquois, had a meeting with 1,100 men, women, and children of the Six Nations council in the field around his home. He tried to persuade them that the British were there for the benefit of the indigenous tribes—to protect them and their land. And he told them that it was in their best interest to help him do that. In an impassioned speech, he told them that his "war kettle is on the fire" and that his weapons were ready for war. He asked them to "take up the hatchet" and join him. However, they were reluctant. They had heard about Braddock's disaster.

In the end, only two hundred agreed to follow King Hendrick and Johnson into battle. When Johnson brought the native warriors with him to the newly built Fort Edward,[48] his militiamen gawked and noted with awe the "juels [sic] in their noses" and "their faces painted with all colors." For many, it was the first time seeing the wild appearance of the warriors up close.

Three days later, Johnson and his men made the twenty-mile trek to the southern shore of Lac du Saint Sacrement. Staring out over her clear waters, Johnson, wanting to "honor his Majesty" King George II, declared the lake had a new name—Lake George.[49]

Having heard sensational reports that there were eight thousand French waiting for him at Crown Point, Johnson was understandably nervous.[50] He set to work building a fort near the water's edge, not only as a place to launch his offensive up the lake but also in a bid to

---

[48] Fort Edward was built on a narrow section of the Hudson River near a portage called the "Great Carrying Place." It was originally called Fort Lyman. Tiny Rogers Island, which is part of the fort enclosure, is considered the "spiritual home" of the US Army Rangers. It was where Robert Rogers wrote his "Ranging Rules" in 1757, which became a guide for irregular military tactics that have been used by armies around the world ever since.

[49] The beauty of Lake George is renowned. Thomas Jefferson called it the "queen of the American lakes."

[50] In reality, there were only about three thousand men at the fort, about the same as Johnson's forces.

defend themselves from what he thought was an overwhelming French force.

At the very north end of the lake, the commander of Fort Saint-Frédéric, Jean-Armand, Baron de Dieskau, had "eyes" on the south end of the lake.[51] As "unreliable" as his Iroquois scouts were (in his words), he did pick up some interesting information—there was a lot of British activity to the south.[52] Suspicious of Johnson's activities, he had two choices—he could wait and see what Johnson was up to, or he could nip any British activity in the bud before the campaign season ended for the winter. Dieskau knew he could not stand idly by as he watched the British prepare to encroach on French territory. Instead of obeying Governor Pierre de Rigaud de Vaudreuil's orders to stay and hold the fort, he decided that another surprise attack was in order.

On September 7th, Johnson received news that the French were on their way, along with seven hundred Native Americans who were said to be "panting for the attack." But their noiseless movements through the woods made it difficult to know where they were. And then additional news reached him—the French were not marching toward his position on Lake George. They were aiming to attack Fort Edward.

Although Johnson said that he "did not dread a surprise," he was disconcerted by the state of his militia at the fort. Hundreds had been ravaged by dysentery, and others suffered under "disorderly management." They were not in prime shape to take on a surprise attack from a large French contingent.

Johnson conferred with King Hendrick. He wanted to split his forces, taking one thousand of his militia and two hundred native warriors through the winding, narrow, hilly path to go protect Fort Edward. The rest would be left behind to continue building the fort.

---

[51] Frédéric is the French name for Crown Point.

Hendrick immediately pointed out the problem of splitting up the forces. He believed it was a tactical mistake, especially on a road with little visibility. Johnson ignored his advice.

At eight the next morning, the eerie silence of the lake descended over the British, with the haunting call of the loons the only sound that broke through. Under Colonel Ephraim Williams Jr. and King Hendrick, the British column moved toward Fort Edward, with the Mohawk chief in the lead.

Dieskau's Mohawk scouts knew every move the British were making and warned him they were on the way to Fort Edward as well. He quickly organized an ambush, knowing the British were unaware of their exact movements. The Kahnawake Mohawk watched silently as the British column passed, waiting to surprise them from the rear.[53] The French regulars were hidden beyond a small rise, and they waited ahead to block any advance while the Canadians flank took the road, ready to rain a hail of musket fire from either side. The British didn't know it, but they had walked right into a trap.

In an unexpected move that stunned his commanders, a French Mohawk warrior was seized by his conscience. He broke orders and called out to King Hendrick. In what Dieskau called "a moment of treachery," the Mohawks had a conversation as hidden French officers looked on in bewilderment and anger. The French-allied Mohawk warrior not only ruined the ambush by revealing himself, but he also tried to convince Hendrick to take his warriors and run, letting the white men fight their own war. The Kahnawake did not want to kill their own people.

Before King Hendrick could respond, a shot reverberated through the forest. The Mohawk leader slowly fell from his horse. He hit the ground, dead. The opening shot of the battle had been taken; the war

---

[52] Lake George is thirty-two miles long from north to south. Given the distance and topography of the lake, it is impossible to visually see from one end to the other.

[53] The Kahnawake Mohawks were a Canadian branch of the Mohawk tribe allied with the French.

was on. At first, the French had the clear advantage of surprise and position. The British Mohawk were also unnerved by the swift death of their leader, which was followed not long after by the death of Colonel Williams.

Johnson, who was still at the lake, could hear the gunfire from three or four miles away. Fearing the worst, he quickly took three hundred men to go to Williams's aid. As the sound of musket fire grew louder, Johnson and his men were met by Williams's retreating militia. Quickly gathering brush, branches, wagons, and anything they could find, they hastily created a barricade on the road. Johnson had brought a cannon with him to back up his defense. Those two quick decisions were what would save him and his militia.

Two hours later, the French regulars came marching in formation toward their barricade, many of their militia bristling with reluctance to face such an entrenched position. Their open position had them at a clear disadvantage, and their fears were not unfounded. Dieskau, however, hardly batted his eye as he led what was practically a suicidal assault.

Though the colonial militia would never be able to match the French army in formation, they performed adequately from behind their protective barrier. As musket fire was exchanged, a large, smoke-filled boom shook the air. Dieskau was taken by surprise by the British cannon. His regulars and their Mohawk allies scattered as they retreated, the heavy artillery firing shot after shot into the thick forest. Scenes of abject horror unfolded as bloody, dismembered limbs were flung about the brush and as disemboweled bodies lay limp.

Once the French salvo was halted by the cannon fire, Johnson's Mohawk warriors leaped over the barricade, whooping with tomahawks in hand. Fierce, close combat went on for several hours, exhausting both sides. The French, who were overwhelmed by Johnson's assault, fell back first, leaving their commander on the field propped up against a tree, riddled with four musket ball wounds. He was now in the hands of the British as their captive. Johnson himself did not fare much better than Dieskau—he was down due to a wound to his groin. The French retreat ended the engagement that came to be known as the Battle of the Bloody Morning Scout. But the fighting was not yet over—the worst was yet to come for the French.

As the wearied French, Canadian, and Mohawk fighters fled, their exhaustion caught up with them. They stopped to catch their breath and rejuvenate themselves at a tiny, forested body of water called Rocky Brook, believing they were safely out of distance from the enemy. They let their guard down, which was a fatal error.

New York Captain William McGinnis snuck through the woods with his two militia regiments to take the resting French contingent by surprise. It worked. The fatigued French fighters were overwhelmed and routed. By the time the skirmish was over, between two hundred and three hundred French lay dead. McGinnis and his men rolled their shot-riddled bodies into Rocky Brook, their seeping blood rendering the quiet pond a grotesque red color. It was hereafter known as Bloody Pond, and the battle ended the group of skirmishes collectively known as the Battle of Lake George. But the picturesque lake had not seen the last of the fighting and bloodshed.

Bloody Pond

Chris Light, CC BY-SA 4.0 <https://creativecommons.org/licenses/by-sa/4.0>, via Wikimedia Commons
https://commons.wikimedia.org/wiki/File:Bloody_Pond_used_by_both_sides_P6250137.jpg

Chapter 8 – The Rules of Battle Change

As 1756 dawned, the rules of war were changing. As Governor Pierre de Rigaud de Vaudreuil wrote to Paris, "wars in this country are very different from the wars of Europe." For the French, it wasn't such a bad thing; in large part, they were the ones changing the rules. Their strategic departure from traditional European battlefield formations to the use of guerilla warfare with the help of native warriors had proven very effective for them. Also, unlike European warfare, they were specifically targeting civilians in a bid to create terror and drive out the British.

The native allies had similar goals and methods. They had been fine with trading with the white men who came across the ocean. They even lived alongside them as friends and neighbors for many years. But as the Europeans encroached on and fought each other for their territory, they could no longer continue the peace. They wanted to discourage more settlers from coming, so they started their own campaigns of terror against the people living on their land.

This was typified in the story of Mary Jemison. She settled in Pennsylvania with her parents and siblings, and she and her Irish family experienced this terror firsthand. A few years after they had settled in America, when Mary was fifteen years old, a group of Shawnee and four Frenchmen came to their home and, unprovoked, attacked the family. The family, who was held captive in their home, spent a terrifying night awaiting their fate. The next day, the very thing Mary spent the night fearing became a reality in front of her eyes. Her parents were brutally massacred and scalped, and her brothers were sent off with the French. The Shawnee men kidnapped Mary and forced her to trek seventy miles over several days. During the night, as the Shawnee sat around the fire preparing the scalps of her family, they told Mary that had the white men never come, this would not have happened. They believed their encroachment had forced them to such extreme and hostile measures.[54] For them, the loss of land and the deaths of their people due to this war were very personal.

The British, however, were used to strict military discipline and rigid battle structures. They did not show the flexibility of the French or the passion of the native nations when it came to battle. It reflected in their losses the year before. Only one of Braddock's targets had been met, and their year ended with one victory, one major loss, and Shirley and Johnson hunkered down, waiting for the action to resume. But they were beginning to realize, late as it was, that they needed to make some changes if they wanted to win.

---

[54] Mary was brought unharmed to a Seneca village and given to two Seneca women who had lost their brother in war. The natives had a custom of taking prisoners to compensate for family members that had been lost in battle. Sometimes the prisoners would be tortured and killed in the most savage way the grieving family could imagine in a bid to satisfy their grief. But in most instances, as in the case of Mary, the prisoner was adopted into the family to replace the deceased relative. Mary said the Seneca women adopted her and treated her very kindly, basically as a sister born from the same mother. She lived a long life with their people as a tribe member and died among them at the age of ninety-one.

Plagued by the colonists' insubordination and desertion, as well as a power struggle between Shirley and Johnson, the British had a number of internal struggles to deal with.[55] But even more detrimental to their victory was the fact that they were slow to realize just how much they needed native allies. As for the French, they may have embraced the guerilla-style warfare that most of their native allies employed, but those fresh from the continent were not ready for the native rules of warfare. These truths were highlighted at the Battle of Fort Oswego, which commenced again in the spring of 1756.

Johnson had sent Captain John Bradstreet and a sizable force to the fort over the winter to shore up its defenses. However, by the spring, the men garrisoned there were in poor shape. The men foolishly brought only a month's worth of supplies with them, and they quickly found themselves in dire straits. No supplies could come over the frozen waters during the winter, and the French ambushed supply lines coming from Albany. In March, the French and their native allies also captured used snowshoes and skates to attack the weakly defended Fort Bull, taking more British food and supplies for themselves.[56]

Having faced months of starvation, the subsequent scurvy, and Native American raids throughout the winter, the fort's commander, Lieutenant Colonel George Mercer, still believed that they could hold the fort. The French, knowing Oswego would be a tougher battle, had concentrated on the weaker forts, but as winter thawed, they turned their attention back to the Great Lakes outpost. It would not fare much better than the unfortunate Fort Bull.

---

[55] Shirley was named Braddock's successor after his death.

[56] The French and natives took the sixty British inside Fort Bull by surprise. Within an hour, the French had killed almost everyone. Those who escaped were caught in the woods and massacred by the French-allied Mohawk and Abenaki warriors. The French then took all the food and supplies they could carry before setting the fort on fire.

In order to kick up their offensive, the French sent forty-four-year-old war veteran Louis-Joseph Marquis de Montcalm over to New England in May 1756.[57] The French were in even higher spirits now, as they had more native allies join them over the winter. This move was triggered when a number of chiefs were killed by the British. Even the steadfastly neutral Iroquois broke their policy, and sixty warriors joined the French. Montcalm, however, began to be disturbed by reports of brutal Native American savagery, even though these attacks were committed against his British enemies.

The British were aware of Montcalm's arrival at Fort Carillon, which was north of Lake George.[58] They began frantic preparations at their fort at the southern end of Lake George in anticipation of a French attack. However, Montcalm had his sights set on Fort Oswego. In early summer, Montcalm prepared the noose and began to tighten it around Fort Oswego. Montcalm snuck up to Montreal in order to sail down the St. Lawrence River with the French regulars and Troupes de Marine. He knew the British were expecting him to attack from the south, so the wily general decided to change the game and defy expectations.

Once he was at Fort Frontenac, Montcalm joined forces with two other commanders. Their combined forces created the largest European army the North American wilderness had seen to date. With war whoops from their native allies, they went to take up their position near Fort Oswego and the two other British forts nearby.[59]

Montcalm's native allies told him that they would not fight in the European style but would keep to the woods in line with the style of fighting they knew best. Montcalm agreed and busied himself getting

---

[57] Montcalm arrived on May 11th. Less than a week later, on May 17th, Britain formally declared war on France, officially beginning the Seven Years' War.

[58] This was a large and important fort guarding the waterway between the northern end of Lake George and the southern end of Lake Champlain.

[59] They were also planning to take the nearby outposts of Fort George and Ontario.

cannons set up on the hill overlooking the fort and digging siege trenches.

The British had been aware of the French advance for a couple of days, and they were frantically trying to fortify the crumbling Fort Ontario. They put a cannon on the roof of a building they thought would be barricaded, but it had to be abandoned when the cannon fire recoil caused the roof under it to collapse. If there was bad foreboding for the fort, this was it.

On August 11th, French commander François-Pierre Rigaud took a group of native warriors and snuck close to the walls of Fort Ontario to snipe the defenders standing atop its crumbling stone. The next day, Fort Ontario felt the full power of the French artillery. A furious barrage of heavy guns and cannon fire from the surrounding cliffs rocked the fort and the men hiding inside. The French had a nearly direct line of fire into the fort from above. Mercer knew there was no way that he and his men could survive this attack.

Taking advantage of a gap in the French siege lines surrounding them, Mercer ordered a daring evacuation of the fort. They would have to leave the fort and cross the river in a bid to make it to Fort Oswego—in broad daylight.

As much as abandoning the fort may have been necessary, they were handing the French a gift in the form of a fortified position that they could use to shoot directly at Fort Oswego. After taking over the abandoned fort, the French trained their heavy guns across the river. As the French began to bombard Oswego's walls with their artillery, Rigaud and his men left Fort Ontario, jumped into the river, and swam toward Forts Oswego and George. They would surround the area to make sure no one could go in or out. The British were trapped.

The British were surrounded and under constant bombardment from the other side of the river. They knew their situation was hopeless. The walls of the fort crumbled more and more after each hit. Little did they know that General Daniel Webb and his men were struggling to reach them, but it would not be in time. After three days of heavy bombardment, there was no choice but to surrender.[60]

Montcalm further insulted the British by forcing them to leave without the traditional war honors.[61] He rejoiced over the impressive wealth he had captured. Besides 1,700 prisoners, he had gained hundreds of bateaux (a kind of boat) as well as a stockpile of artillery and munitions. His native allies, on the other hand, seethed with anger. They waited eagerly for the chance to strip the British prisoners of their personal effects, but Montcalm would not allow it.

Angry, they took matters into their own hands. Some rushed into the hospital, mercilessly killing and stripping the wounded prisoners as they lay in their beds. Others tried to reach the prisoners under French guard. As some British tried to flee the fort, Abenaki chased them down and killed them with blows from their tomahawks.[62, 63] No one was spared. Every British soul they could lay their hands on, even women, children, and babies, were killed or captured.

The native warriors were bent on taking plunder and captives back to their villages in a show of honor and proof of their victory. However, what they see as honor, Montcalm saw as barbaric. This was nothing like the civilized European codes of war that he was used to.

As much as the British were his enemy, he could not bear the thought of what the native warriors might do to the one hundred men

---

[60] There were many women and children inside the fort as well.

[61] A ceremony where the enemy is allowed to march from their fort and lay down their arms as a way to show them honor and appreciation for their valor in fighting. However, Montcalm, even though he was very staunch in sticking to the etiquette of surrender, refused the British this honor. He believed that Lieutenant Colonel John Littlehales, who took over command when Mercer was killed by French mortar shells, should have put up more of a fight and so did not earn any war honors.

[62] Some French soldiers, drunk on the barrels of rum found in the fort, followed suit and also killed the fleeing British.

[63] Not even Littlehales escaped this brutality. A group of Abenaki warriors grabbed hold of him and beat him near death, saying he was a "coward and had behaved ill" because of his "quick" surrender.

they captured if they did not get the ransoms they were seeking. He offered his own money to ransom them to ensure they didn't meet a horrific end. Although he downplayed the savagery in his report back to Paris, Montcalm vowed he would never again allow this to happen. But that vow would prove to be meaningless.

Montcalm trying to stop the massacre of the British.

https://commons.wikimedia.org/wiki/File:Montcalm_trying_to_stop_the_massacre.jpg

Chapter 9 – The Tragic End of Fort William Henry

By 1757, the war clouds had again gathered over Lake George. Though Montcalm and the French were busy for the remainder of 1756, they had not forgotten about the fort that Johnson and the British built on the southern end of Lake George. If Montcalm could take the now fully built Fort William Henry from the British, the French would control all thirty-two miles of Lake George. It was the next link in the French bid to control the entire series of waterways that linked the Atlantic Ocean near New York City to the northern Atlantic outside of Hudson Bay in east-central Canada.[64]

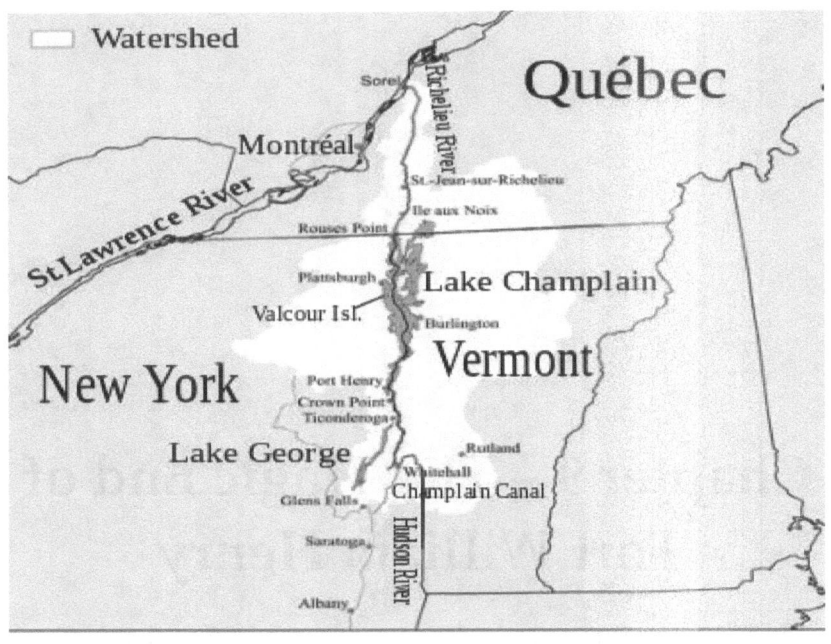

Important waterways fought over by the French and British.

Champlainmap.png: Kmusser / derivative work: Pierre cb, CC BY-SA 2.5 <https://creativecommons.org/licenses/by-sa/2.5>, via Wikimedia Commons https://commons.wikimedia.org/wiki/File:Champlainmap.svg

While Montcalm was gathering troops at Fort Carillon in preparation for an all-out assault down the lake, General Webb sat virtually idle in Fort William Henry. It was not due to a lack of information—he constantly got reports about French activity, and it

---

[64] Known today as the Trans Adirondack Water Route, the chain goes from the Hudson River to Lake George, then to Lake Champlain via the La Chute River. It then goes from Lake Champlain to the Richelieu River and then to the St. Lawrence River. From the St. Lawrence River, it goes to the Gulf of St. Lawrence, which eventually spills out into the Northern Atlantic. This was the most strategically important chain to both the British and the French, as it would allow them to easily move men, weapons, supplies, and goods through the New York wilderness. Much of the fighting was done between the forts that guarded these waterways, including Fort Edward on the Hudson River, which was several miles southeast of Lake George.

was fairly obvious that the French were going to launch an attack. Webb just chose not to do anything about it. He and John Campbell, Earl of Loudoun, who was now the commander of the British forces in North America, didn't believe Montcalm would be foolish enough to launch an attack over the iced lake during winter. Montcalm himself thought it was a waste of time and energy.

However, even though it went against Montcalm's advice, Governor Vaudreuil was determined to launch a surprise winter attack on Fort William Henry. Rigaud was given command of the mission, and he took three columns of soldiers and skirted the frozen west shore of the lake. Men went ahead of the columns and poked the ice with picks to check its thickness and how safe it was to walk across.

Rigaud intended to surprise the fort, but he did not seem to realize the sounds of their footsteps crunching across the snowy frozen lake and the strikes of their ice picks carried down the lake. Their approach was no surprise to those in the fort.

The British called everyone into the fort, and the French, unable to do much else, burned their outbuildings and three hundred bateaux sitting on the shore. Determined to complete his mission, Rigaud and his men attempted to take the fort. But they were missing an important component to victory—heavy artillery. Without it, their feeble attempts fell flat. When a late March blizzard dumped three feet of snow on Rigaud and his men, their four-day siege ended, and they retreated back to Fort Carillon. With a weak, not-so-surprise attack like this, it was no wonder Webb felt secure sitting behind the fort's walls. But the lake would eventually thaw.

Despite the failed winter assault, Fort William Henry remained too tempting to the French. They would mount another attack with a bit of an advantage—the British had been dragging their feet about repairing the outbuildings burned over the winter. This allowed the French to concentrate their full might on the fort walls.

By mid-July, the British were getting nervous about what the French were doing at Fort Carillon. In order to find out, Colonel John

Parker and 350 men paddled north up the lake. Unfortunately for them, the French were already one step ahead. Almost as soon as the British boats had hit the water, the French knew about it. All they had to do was wait.

The next morning, the three boats that Parker had sent ahead were set upon by Ensign de Corbiere and 450 men, mostly native warriors. After taking men captive and bringing them ashore, the French were able to extract information from the British. They found out that Parker and the rest of their contingent were planning to land at Sabbath Day Point, a little more than halfway between the two forts.

When Parker and his fleet rounded the point the next day, they saw their own boats by the shore, leading Parker to believe they had reached the rendezvous point safely. But when they got closer to shore, they were stunned by a hail of musket fire from where the French and natives were lying in wait. Before the British could retreat, they were quickly surrounded by fifty canoes. As they tried to flee, the French opened fire, the sound of gunshots reverberating between the mountains on either side of the lake. The French-allied natives jumped into the waters and, with surprising agility and ferocity, chased down the rest. Cries of the wounded and those being overturned could be heard across the serene waters as the warriors capsized or dragged their vessels under. Those who fell in the water were "speared like fish" or drowned. Only one hundred of Parker's men survived, with many being taken captive and brought to Fort Carillon.

To their horror, the captives were not treated according to the European code of war etiquette—they were in the hands of the natives, who played by different rules. The unfortunate prisoners had ropes tied around their necks and were forced to walk to the camp outside of the fort. As the day wore on and as the natives freely drank the British rum they had confiscated, their ferocity increased, leading to the shocking instance of one prisoner being boiled and eaten. Any information the British gained had come at a devastating price.

There was now no doubt in the minds of the British that another attack on Fort William Henry was imminent. British regulars and colonial militiamen gathered at the fort in a bid to try to defend it. They hastily built additional timber and brush barricades around the fort walls for an extra layer of protection. The men waited, not knowing when the French might arrive.

General Webb then stunned the officers of the fort when he left them, hurrying back to Fort Edward. He gave command of the fort to Lieutenant Colonel George Monro. His final words to Monro must have chilled the officer to his core. He told Monro "to make the best [surrender] terms left in your power." His belief in the fort's imminent defeat, though perhaps realistic, must have been highly unsettling.

By the time Webb left, Monro had 2,300 men to fight for the fort—technically. These numbers are frightfully deceiving. Only one thousand of the men gathered were in fighting condition; the rest were plagued with injuries or illness. On the other end of the lake, Montcalm's force of 9,200 was in prime shape and ready for battle.[65]

The first indications that the French forces were on their way came during the night of August 2nd. Bonfires could be seen on the shore farther up the lake, burning brightly against the pitch-black silhouette of the mountains.

When day dawned on August 3rd, the British were awakened by the booming of French cannons. Though they were not in range of the fort, the French were announcing that they had arrived and were heavily armed. A fuller picture of what was coming emerged for the fort's inhabitants. They could see bateaux tied together to create large pontoons carrying French cannons and heavy artillery coming down the lake.

It was easy to see the French had landed along the shore only a half-mile from the fort, outside of the range of fire. Shortly after, the clanging sound of French shovels could be heard, the noise carrying across the water. They wasted no time building trenches, digging their way toward the fort. Within a short time, the British were under siege.

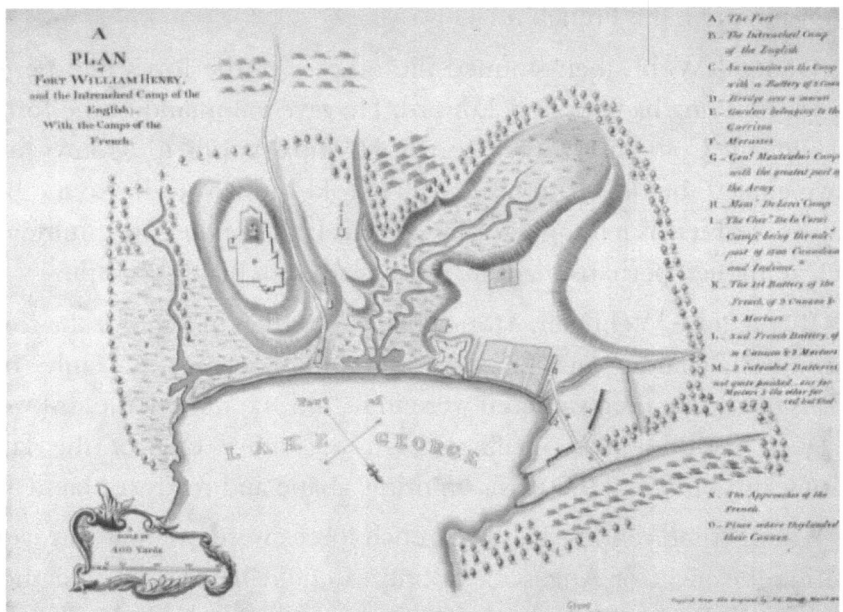

Fort William Henry and surrounding landscape Library of Congress

https://commons.wikimedia.org/wiki/File:Plan_du_si%C3%A8ge_de_fort_William_Henry_en_1757.jpg

Montcalm and his men furiously rushed to set up their defenses along the lakeshore. The star-shaped outpost was strategically located on a twenty-foot hill with the lake in front and swampy marshland around two other sides, forming a sort of wetland moat. But as well

---

[65] Sixteen hundred of these were native warriors, gathered from 33 different tribes. In preparation for taking Fort William Henry, Montcalm had gone on one of the biggest French campaigns to gather Native American allies. He promised them that they could ransom British prisoners and that the British fort was "swimming in brandy" for the taking. Montcalm's contingent also consisted of Canadian Troupes de Marine, the toughest fighters in the army.

constructed as its thirty-foot thick walls were, complacency remained a constant enemy.

This was where Monro made his first mistake in being distracted and reacting to only what he could see. As they busily fortified the fort from the lakeside, Monro was unaware that three thousand French soldiers and natives had snuck up behind the fort and were deeply garrisoned in the woods at their back. They set to work cutting off the road to Fort Edward. The British didn't know it yet, but they were already surrounded.

Once Monro found out that they were surrounded, he knew his situation was desperate, maybe even more desperate than he had anticipated. Webb's final words may have rung in his ears, but he was not ready to do himself and the fort the dishonor of surrendering without firing a shot. He believed that if he asked Webb for reinforcements—the men at Fort Edward were sitting only sixteen miles away—the general could not turn down the request. Messengers were sent out, and Monro waited confidently for help to arrive. He just needed to hold the fort for a few more days until help arrived.

Before their classic European-style battle even began, the French tried to break the British down with psychological warfare. French soldiers and native warriors shot at the walls of the fort day and night, hidden in the dense trees around the fort. As the French dug trenches closer to the walls, snipers followed the path, getting close enough to shoot soldiers on top of the wall. Though the British on the wall were able to defend and hold the snipers back, their unfortunate oxen outside of the walls were easy targets. One hundred dead animal carcasses soon littered the grounds around the fort walls, and the French and their allies continued to relentlessly fire on the fort for five days.

Montcalm was confident that he had the victory. As a man bound by war etiquette, he would prefer to take the doomed fort without further bloodshed. Walking under the red flag of truce and accompanied by drummers and fifteen grenadiers, Montcalm's aide-de-camp Louis de Bougainville marched to the fort to meet with Monro.[66] The French would offer a peaceful surrender.

Bougainville was greeted civilly at the gates of the fort, but he was blindfolded before being taken to Monro. Once in the commander's presence, his blindfold was removed. He formally and politely informed Monro that the French were calling upon them to abandon the fort on what they considered to be their territory.

The French would give Monro just one hour to decide the fate of the fort. Offering added incentive to answer on time and answer correctly, Bougainville warned, "Once our batteries are in place and the cannons are fired, perhaps there would not be time, nor would it be in our power to restrain the cruelties of a mob of Indians." The menacing message was clear—surrender, or we will not restrain our native allies, and we will not be responsible for the savagery that they inflict.

Bougainville drove home the point by reminding the commander of the bloody massacre the British had suffered at the hands of native warriors after the fall of Fort Oswego. Surely Monro would not want the same fate to befall him and the men, women, and children inside his fort.

As if reinforcing Bougainville's words, an Abenaki warrior came near the fort walls and shouted a menacing message to the British in French, "Ah, you won't surrender. Well fire first...then take care to defend yourself because if I capture you, you will get no quarter." Failure to surrender would mean there would be no mercy in defeat.

Under the rules of European warfare, Monro was fully expected to surrender since his defeat was certain. However, he did not want to give up with reinforcements expected at any moment. The fort was too important to give up, and he would continue to defend it until

---

[66] The French flag was white, so they used red to denote messengers coming in a peaceful fashion.

General Webb sent reinforcements. He did not need the full hour to make his decision.

Monro bluffed, telling Bougainville that he could not surrender because his orders were to hold the fort. Putting on a brave front, he then told the Frenchman that the barbarity of the natives does not scare him. He told them, win or lose, they would fight down to the last man. But despite his show of bravado, Monro was extremely nervous. He sent more messages to Webb, letting him know the situation was becoming increasingly dire and begging him to send help quickly.

After receiving the refusal to surrender, Montcalm continued his dig toward the fort, setting up his cannons for heavy bombardment. Monro's men frantically fired cannons and guns at the advancing French. Even if they couldn't stop them, they needed to at least slow them down until help or news from Webb arrived from Fort Edward. They just needed to hang on a little longer. Little did they know that General Webb had already sent a messenger with his reply; he would just never reach them.

The situation became grimmer for the fort over the next few days. Although fire was exchanged back and forth, and while the British, for the most part, were able to keep the French at bay, they could not sustain this siege for long, especially once the French cannons were positioned and ready.

On August 6th, cannon fire cut through the air on both sides, the deafening sounds echoing between the lake's mountains in a constant cacophony. Howitzers shook the ground, and muskets sent a hail of metal toward the fort. Although the sand beneath the fort's logs helped to dampen the blows, French artillery soon started to devastate its walls. Mortar shells were lobbed over the walls, and the casualties began to mount.

Casualties were not just coming from outside the walls either. Four British cannons and a mortar gun exploded behind the walls, killing the men around it. The British were in as much danger from their own cannons as they were from those of the French.

Desperately, Montcalm ordered that the roofs of the barracks and other buildings be quickly ripped off to prevent fires from starting or spreading around the fort when hit by mortar shells. When French fire stopped for the night, Montcalm and his men could be heard, though not seen, digging their way to the walls in the dark. It was just another masterful piece of psychological warfare on the part of the French.

On August 7th, mortar fire tore a hole through the British flag flying over the fort. The carpenter who was sent to fix it was killed immediately by incoming fire. Sensing this as a symbolism of their doom, morale inside the fort tumbled. The symbolism of it was not lost on the French either. Knowing the fort was lost, Montcalm halted the barrage and again sent an offer of surrender under the red flag of truce.

Bougainville again approached the gates and told the sentries that he had a letter for Monro. When Monro opened the letter, he expected to read the terms of surrender. Instead, his heart sank in horror. The letter, stained red with blood, was from General Webb. Several days before, a Mohawk scout named Kanectagon was lying in wait next to the road to Fort Edward, waiting for someone whom he could capture and ransom. His patience was rewarded when the messenger with a letter from General Webb passed by. A Frenchman who was traveling with Kanectagon searched the British soldier and found the letter in a secretly sewn pocket in the dead man's coat.

When Montcalm was given the letter, he was overjoyed. It was the best news he could have hoped for. And not only that, he could use it to his advantage. Wanting to destroy any hopes Monro had left, he sent the letter with Bougainville, along with the letter of surrender.

A tornado of thoughts must have swirled through Monro's mind as he read Webb's words. The general succinctly wrote that he did not think it "prudent" to send more soldiers to the besieged fort and that

Monro should try to get the best terms of surrender possible.[67] There would be no rescue from Fort Edward, and the news was reaching Monro devastatingly late.

Monro next read the letter of surrender, which was what he was expecting. The French hoped the blow of Webb's letter would be devastating enough to get Monro to surrender. Monro looked up at Bougainville and told him that the French had been a most pleasant enemy. Yet his next words shocked the Frenchman. Monro told him that he could not yet surrender. The walls of the fort had not yet been breached, and if he surrendered now, it would be a terrible dishonor.[68]

Though the British had spent five sleepless days and nights defending their fort and waiting for reinforcements that would never come, they would continue to fight until the walls of their fort crumbled. As the French recommenced their salvo, morale inside the fort was shattered. Although the walls were still standing, the situation was utterly hopeless. The militia fighters were not only exhausted but also traumatized. They were running out of food and munitions, and their artillery was succumbing to metal fatigue, creating a higher chance that they could explode each time another shot was fired. With no help coming, surrender was the only option left.

Montcalm's terms of surrender were carefully crafted so as to avoid the fiasco of Fort Oswego, where the natives took scalps and captives. Montcalm promised the British they could leave the fort unbothered by the French native allies, although they could only take their personal items. Everything else would become French property, which would be sent to supply their Canadian forts. But the native warriors wanted their share of the spoils, so the French made a deal

---

[67] Webb knew that the fort was almost sure to fall to the French. When that happened, Fort Edward would be the only outpost held by the British in this important region. If he took soldiers from Fort Edward, he would leave it too poorly defended if the French tried to take it after Fort William Henry fell.

[68] Monro was following the European military code of honor, which stated that until the fort walls were actually breached, it would be a dishonor to surrender, inferring that there was cowardice on the part of its commander.

with them that if they left the departing British alone, they could have whatever was leftover at the fort.

On August 9th, at 7 o'clock in the morning, the white flag of surrender was raised over the fort. The British would negotiate the terms of surrender. As per their custom, the French terms were rather generous to the British. Among other things, they would be allowed to leave the fort with honors and with a guarantee that the French would not allow their native allies to harm or harass them on their way out. It was a complete contrast to the fiasco of Fort Oswego.

However, the native chiefs allied with the French did feel that the terms were generous toward them. They had been left out of the surrender negotiations altogether. Montcalm gathered them and informed them that under the terms of surrender, they were not permitted to take captives, pillage, or strip the defeated enemy as they left the fort. Although the chiefs listened politely to Montcalm, it belied the anger that boiled up inside of them. They cared nothing for the European code of honor—their honor was dependent on returning home with captives and spoils. It was the only reason they had agreed to fight. They felt betrayed by the French, who were now going back on the promises they had made when recruiting the warriors. They had sacrificed their fighters to the war and now were getting nothing in return. It was humiliating.

The tribal warriors were further insulted when Monroe threw a banquet for Montcalm and his officers, graciously toasting them as worthy opponents. The native fighters had not been asked to join this peaceful gathering, essentially treating them as if they had been of little consequence in the battle. It also raised fears that should the white men on both sides become friendly, they might decide to come together against their people. The Native Americans could see no upside to having allied themselves with the French in this war.

When the fort was officially handed over to the French at noon, trouble began brewing immediately. The British soldiers laid down their weapons and marched out of the fort walls to an encampment not far away, but many of their people still remained inside the fort.

Soon after they left the fort, screams from behind them pierced the air. Native warriors, intent on taking spoils and captives, had forced their way past the French guards and made their way into the fort. The French soldiers tried in vain to stop them. The warriors pillaged, drank until they were drunk and angry, and terrorized the British prisoners. One ran out of the area where the wounded were held, grasping "a human head, from which trickled streams of blood."

Montcalm desperately tried to get the situation under control, but due to the many languages spoken by the various tribesmen and a sad lack of interpreters, communication was nearly impossible. He was going to have to find a way to get the British out of the fort, and quickly.

He devised a plan to spirit the British away from the fort during the night. The French hoped that under cover of darkness, the fort's inhabitants could safely leave while the native warriors slept. That plan did not go over well.

As they were leaving, the warriors woke up. Upon realizing what was happening, they swarmed the French encampment and angrily threatened their officers. The British were brought back to the fort. They would have to leave in daylight so as not to further anger the French allies.

When the sun dawned over the mountains on the eastern side of the lake on August 10th, the British began their march out of the fort under their mortar-torn flag. Escorted by French grenadiers, the well-organized British regulars marched out first, followed by a disorderly line of the colonial militia. Camp followers brought up the rear.[69] All were unarmed.

---

[69] These were women who stayed with the soldiers to help with chores, such as sewing, cooking, and laundry.

The tension was thick. The French could feel it, and it worried them. As the grenadiers escorted the column away from the fort, the natives had already begun to make their move. They broke back into the camp, killing and scalping the wounded left behind.

The disillusioned native warriors care nothing for the terms of surrender given by the French. The French promises to the British meant as little as their promises to them. And trying to sneak the British out from under their noses had further antagonized them. They went ahead of the British and laid in wait on the side of the road leading out from the fort. They were determined to take the spoils that were their due.

With terrifying war whoops, they launched themselves from their hiding places and set upon the regulars in front. They took what they wanted, including Monro's horse. The French, who were nervous about what might happen and wanting to avoid more bloodshed, advised the British to just give the warriors what they wanted and to not put up a fight. Monro urgently passed the message down the column as the warriors took everything they had, including their hats.

Understandably, the column began to panic. They expected the terms of surrender to be adhered to and that they would peacefully march to Fort Edward. This turn of events was shocking and frightening. The situation had surprisingly and quickly spiraled out of control. But as frightening as it was for the regulars in the front, they had actually been relatively lucky. The situation became far more terrifying for those following behind.

Not content with taking what few belongings they had, the warriors quickly surrounded the militiamen and the women and children following behind. The ever-dreaded "hell whoop" rang out, signaling a massacre. With ferocity and without restraint, the warriors took hatchets and tomahawks and leaped at the men, killing and taking scalps as trophies of war. Hundreds were taken off as captives, many with the intent of being ransomed back in Canada. One hundred and eighty-five people who had left the fort lay dead along the road.[70, 71]

The attack lasted just a few minutes, but it was intensely terrifying. When Montcalm heard what was happening, he personally rushed to the scene. By the time he got there, it was over. Monro was courageously rescuing captives, some of whom had lost all their clothes and were brought back stark naked.[72]

When General Webb found out about the surrender, he sent five hundred men to meet those on their way to Fort Edward. Expecting to see an orderly column calmly marching down the "King's Road," the soldiers were shocked to see thirty of their people crashing out of the woods and running down the hill toward them, many without shirts or even pants.

Montcalm had lost his native allies and had a lot of explaining to do as to how this massacre occurred despite his orders. He would not pursue a seizure of Fort Edward. He had worse things to worry about. Word spread about how the French treated their native allies, making it highly unlikely that new warriors could be recruited. Those already allied with the French broke or threatened to break their alliance in the wake of the battle.

The easily won French victory, which had relied so heavily on native warriors, was now leading the French to their greatest crisis. Without their native allies, they would find that winning North

---

[70] Numbers of those killed vary. Original sources said 1,500 were killed, but the report was likely sensationalized to spark outrage among New Englanders. After much research, scholars believe the dead was actually 185, though some sources say as low as 75 or 85.

[71] Though the book is highly fictionalized, this event is the foundation for James Fenimore Cooper's *The Last of the Mohicans*.

[72] After taking anything of value from the fort, the French burned it to the ground. Today, Fort William Henry has been rebuilt as a museum on the hill adjacent to its original location.

America would be out of their grasp. The many battles they had won over the past few years would all be for naught.

Chapter 10 – The Battle on Snowshoes and the Legend of Rogers Rock

The year 1758 started off with a lesser-known battle that would become local folklore centuries later. In late February, still the dead of winter, the British decided to cancel their planned attacks on Fort Carillon (Ticonderoga) and Crown Point. Instead of sitting idly by, they would send out a reconnaissance mission headed by Captain Robert Rogers, the smart, fearless, and cunning founder of the Army Rangers. Rogers was to take four hundred of his Army Rangers to scout out the situation just north of the forts.

In the days before he left Fort Edward, he found out that the fort's commander, Lieutenant Colonel William Haviland, had made his mission public to everyone in the fort. Rogers was angered that a security breach could compromise his mission. He was further angered to find out a few days later that a servant at the fort was captured in a French and Native American ambush. He felt sure the man had talked and revealed his mission. Although he felt that his mission was compromised and the French knew he was coming, he prepared to set out anyway.[73]

Rogers faced another setback on the day he was supposed to leave. Instead of 400 men, Haviland was allowing him to take just 184, including officers. Rogers argued that since he was sure the French knew he was coming, he would need *more* men, not less. Haviland didn't budge on the issue, and Rogers found his decision incomprehensible in the face of the situation. Still, he had no choice but to bitterly obey his orders.

The second day of Rogers's journey, March 11th, saw him and his men march past the depressing sight of the burned-out Fort William Henry. The men could not take the time to dwell on the past defeat and its aftermath. They donned ice cleats and started their long haul over the frozen waters, making it about a third of the way up the lake by the end of the day.

The first sign of danger appeared the next day, and it ran across the lake on four legs. The Rangers spotted a dog coming from one of the small islands in the lake—a sure sign that native warriors were nearby.[74] Scouts on ice skates were sent to check out the situation.

Though they could see no one, Rogers did not want to take any chances, as the native warriors were masters of hiding and ambushing. He and his men hurried into the densely wooded shoreline and exchanged their ice cleats for snowshoes—they would move where they had more cover. Just to be sure, they would wait until night to continue their trek.

Over the next couple of days, they marched in snowshoes during the night, resting in the frigid cold and the deep snow of the woods during the day without the warmth of a fire so they would not give their position away. When they did move, the unnatural gait required

---

[73] Rogers did not appear in any French reports or sources until after his mission, making it very unlikely that the French knew about his mission.

[74] It was commonly known that Native American raiding parties took dogs with them.

to walk on the snowshoes slowed them down. The cold and the journey quickly took their toll on the men, causing considerable fatigue as they pushed through the snow.

On March 13th, Rogers stopped his men within a few miles of a French advanced post and, after conferring with his officers, made a plan. But what he didn't plan for was what was actually happening at Fort Carillon the day before.

French Marines, along with two hundred Iroquois and Nipissing warriors, had arrived at the fort to help defend it. That night, the warriors held council and had their medicine man speak. Unaware that Rogers and his men were in the area, he delivered a shocking prophecy—a British war party was already near. By the time the news reached the Marine commander Sieur de La Durantaye, native scouts had come back with a report that seemed to confirm the medicine man's words. They had come across the tracks of two hundred men with snowshoes, and scouts at the top of Bald Mountain could see soldiers moving into the area—it was the foretold British war party. Fort Carillon sent out three parties of French militiamen and native warriors to meet them.

Rogers expected the French to come across the ice, so he brought his men inland, trudging between Bald Mountain and Trout Brook through four feet of snow. Before long, advanced guards sent back news—the French had been spotted. They did not know it was only one of the parties that had been sent out, and so they spread themselves along the river to meet the ninety-seven Frenchmen and natives coming their way.

Once the French contingent passed in front of their left wing, Rogers took the first shot. Caught by surprise, the first volley killed forty of the French-allied natives. The rest retreated. The first confrontation had been a success for Rogers—he had played the French and native game of ambush and won. However, Rogers had no idea that the other two French units were waiting to ambush *them*.

Not wanting to allow those fleeing to regroup, Ensign Gregory MacDonald and Captain Charles Bulkeley took their respective divisions and set off in hot pursuit. Little did they realize they were chasing them back to their larger French contingent and straight into mortal danger.

The triumphant Rangers, who were exhilarated from their recent victory, ran straight into Ensign Jean-Baptiste de Langy and his men, their guns at the ready. The French opened fire at close range, catching the Rangers by surprise. The Rangers could hardly react before Bulkeley and all his officers were on the ground, dead or wounded. MacDonald and another officer, though mortally wounded, rallied their men who were still standing and led them back to Rogers and the main column.

Rogers and his men were unaware that their compatriots were in dire straits. They were combing the area of their victorious ambush, scalping and stripping the dead. The scattered Rangers were caught off guard and were out of battle-ready formation when the French swarmed in on their right flank. Rogers was able to think quickly on his feet, and he immediately ordered his men toward the higher ground of Bald Mountain. There, they would either shake the French or die making their last stand.

The French, hot in pursuit, were not about to give up that easily. The hated Rogers and his Rangers had been a serious thorn in their side.[75] They could not let this chance to rid themselves of such troublesome enemies while they were within their reach slip away.

Rogers and his men fought fiercely as they were pushed higher and higher up the mountainside. Greatly outnumbered, Rogers and his men resorted to woodland fighting tactics, something they were quite experienced with. They were able to hold the French advance back for some time, but they could not hold out forever. British Lieutenant

---

[75] Rogers specialized and was an expert at harassing the French, even boldly and brazenly jumping into the trenches around Fort Carillon and taking prisoners from right under the noses of the rest of the garrison.

William Phillips and his men fought to guard the rear, but their small unit was slowly surrounded.

Some of Phillips's unit was able to break away and escape, but Phillips, who had been promised protection by the French if they surrendered, had little choice but to capitulate. However, when the native warriors found the scalps of their dead tribesmen on the surviving soldiers, they became enraged. There were no French promises that could hold them back from taking revenge. After tying Phillips and his men to trees, the natives took out their fury on them. Only three of them would survive.[76] As brutal as it was, their surrender bought Rogers some time and allowed him and the rest of his men to get away for the moment.

Rogers's last-ditch effort to get to the high ground was not without sacrifice. Fifty men were lost as they scrambled up the mountain, but Rogers, with less than 120 men, many of whom were wounded, continued their difficult ascent up the snow-covered slope. Most of them would not make it.

As darkness neared, Rogers hoped to hold out until he could make a nighttime escape with the twenty men he had left with him. The French, on the other hand, were desperate not to lose them to the night. They caught up to Rogers; they came so close that hand-to-hand combat nearly started. Defeat and likely death were close at hand for the British.

It was now time for Rogers to follow his own advice that he set out in his "Ranging Rules." One rule states that "If the enemy is so superior that you are in danger of being surrounded by them, let the whole body disperse, and everyone take a different route to the place of rendezvous appointed." If possible, one should hold firm and wait until night to escape. Now was the time.

---

[76] Phillips and the two other survivors were eventually taken north by the native warriors and paraded around their villages in a show of victory. Phillips endured a number of harrowing experiences before escaping and making it back to the British army. The fate of the other survivors remains unknown.

The Rangers each scattered into the gloom of the mountain, hoping to hide until nightfall and then make for the rendezvous point. With the natives in close pursuit, not everyone was able to escape; some were taken as prisoners. Rogers, however, made what became a legendary escape.

Throwing off his coat, Rogers fled through the woods along the flat mountaintop. The French, believing him dead, gave up trying to find his body. However, the Iroquois warriors persisted. Rogers made it to the eastern side of the mountain but stopped dead in his tracks. Looking down, he saw a precipitous slope leading seven hundred feet down to the frozen lake. He was trapped. But he was also crafty.

Taking off his snowshoes, he turned them around and tied them on backward, walking away from the edge and back into the woods. He hoped to make it look like his escape ended at the cliff's edge. When the Iroquois pursued his tracks later, they found two sets of snowshoe prints ending at the edge and assumed that Rogers went over the side.[77]

Rogers Rock.

Internet Archive Book Images, No restrictions, via Wikimedia Commons https://commons.wikimedia.org/wiki/File:A_battle_fought_on_snow_shoes_-_Rogers%27_Rock,_Lake_George,_March_13,_1758_(1917)_(14596080357).jpg

---

[77] This cliff face is now famously known as Rogers Rock.

A little while later, the native warriors saw a sight that greatly frightened them. There was Rogers, whom they had assumed died going over the cliff, running across the frozen lake. They reasoned that no regular man could have survived the drop to the lake and believed that Rogers could have only survived with the help of spirits. Believing that he had supernatural support behind him, the Iroquois refused to pursue him any further.[78]

Rogers managed to rendezvous with the other survivors at the point near the lake where they left their packs and sleds. Messengers on ice skates were sent to Fort Edward to let them know what had happened and to get help in bringing the wounded back. After spending two nights on the frigid, wind-whipped Sloop Island in the middle of the frozen lake, Rogers and his defeated men dragged themselves into Fort Edward on March 15th.

For his courage and leadership, Rogers was shortly thereafter promoted to major. The French would soon find out how wrong they were about his death when he reconstructed his shattered Army Rangers and took them to Crown Point to continue harassing the garrison.

---

[78] Local folklore tells a fantastic legend of Rogers sliding down the rock face to the lake and escaping, his slide being what cleared the slope of its vegetation. This is no doubt taken from the Iroquois belief about what happened, but surviving such an escape down the icy slope would have been virtually impossible. Rogers did not give an account of his escape in his narrative, but the story of his escape has been pieced together by various reports and probabilities.

Chapter 11 – A British Victory and a Humiliating Disaster

Up until June of 1758, the British had suffered one demoralizing and humiliating defeat after another, with a few exceptions. Part of the problem lay with the trouble brewing from within.

The commander of the British army in North America, John Campbell, Earl of Loudoun, had faced nothing but years of problems from colonial assemblies, with Massachusetts being a particularly sharp thorn in his side.

The colonists continued to argue for the same rights as British citizens living over in the homeland—they considered themselves subjects of the Crown as well. They just happened to live on the other side of the ocean. Why should they be treated differently than any other citizen of Britain? In protest, they began refusing to pay taxes imposed by England. They reasoned that if they were not afforded the same rights and protections as citizens, then they were not obligated to pay taxes.

Loudoun was not used to being defied, and he was flummoxed over why the colonists were so rebellious. He could not understand their valid fears. The colonists realized they were obligated to wage war for empires that did not consider them citizens. This risked bankrupting their fragile economy, and in addition, their tenuous grasp on the rights they did have might be taken away at any time. Issues over money and morals heavily divided the colonists from the British. But instead of acknowledging their concerns, Loudoun only viewed colonial Americans as troublesome rebels.

London saw the issues and problems mounting, prompting the government to fire Loudoun as the commander. The man to take his place, Lord William Pitt, was much more astute when it came to dealing with the colonists. He knew that no matter how demanding or headstrong they were, he absolutely needed them in order to win this war. And to win the war, he must first win over the colonists.

He started by having money sent over for the army—a smart move considering that the military salaries were a point of contention for the colonists. Feeling that some of their concerns had been addressed and heard, the colonists were elated and more willing to cooperate. Whereas it had previously been incredibly difficult to get militiamen to enlist, they were now signing up by the thousands. Pitt's strategy worked, and it was the first step toward turning things around.

Despite their issues, the British never took their eyes off their goal—control of the New York route and, ultimately, Canada. But in order to do that, they would have to do what seemed nearly impossible—defeat a sizable French force at the formidable Fort Carillon.

To round out their plan for Canadian domination, they planned to take Fort Louisbourg and Fort Frontenac in Canada, as well as make a second attempt on Fort Duquesne. A major offensive aimed at crushing the French was about to begin.

The first offensive movement began in June when Major General Jeffery Amherst seriously outmanned the French by bringing eleven thousand soldiers up against the three thousand men garrisoned at Fort Louisbourg. After landing at Cape Breton, Nova Scotia, the British easily took Lighthouse Point.

Fort Louisbourg.

Pierre-Charles Canot, CC0, via Wikimedia Commons
https://commons.wikimedia.org/wiki/File:Pierre-Charles_Canot_-_Views_of_Montreal_and_Louisburg,_A_View_of_Louisburg_in_North_America_taken_near_the_Light_House_-_B2001.2.1498_-_Yale_Center_for_British_Art.jpg

From the point, the British army launched a punishing 49-day assault, bombarding the besieged fortress with cannons from land while 157 British ships silently sailed into the harbor and decimated the entire French fleet. It was a crippling dual assault, and with their fort ablaze, the French had no choice but to surrender.

When the French finally surrendered the fort on July 26th, 1758, the British showed that they had not forgotten the tragedy of Fort William Henry. The French were accorded no honors of war, and all those who had fought against them were taken prisoner. To complete their seizure of the region, all eight thousand inhabitants of Cape Breton Island were deported back to France. The British had their first real victory in years, and they were one step closer to their goal of taking over Canada. However, things were not going as well farther south at Fort Carillon, where the bloodiest battle of the war raged.

Under Brigadier Lord George Howe and Major General James Abercrombie, the British were preparing to take on Fort Carillon in early July. They had high hopes for Howe's leadership; according to his fellow officers, he was considered "the best soldier in the British army." But would he be enough to take on Montcalm and his seemingly impenetrable fortress?

The British were taking no chances. They gathered one of their largest forces—fifteen thousand men and eighteen siege cannons—believing that their much larger force was assured of victory. But they were about to find out that larger numbers did not necessarily equate to an easy victory, nor did it assure any victory at all.

On July 5th, with a fleet of one thousand small boats, the British set off, heading up the lake as the sun crept over the eastern mountain range. Their many boats covered the width of the lake, dotting the waters from the eastern shore of the lake clear to the western shore. Bagpipes and bugle music danced across the waters and echoed among the hills. The colorful coats and banners of the British, Scottish Highlanders, and colonial militia created a brilliant pageant the likes of which the lake had never seen before nor would see again.

Before Montcalm could even see their fleet, he knew the British were coming and that they were coming strong. Lookouts on top of Roger's Rock saw the incredible flotilla silently rowing their way, and they ran to report to Montcalm. He knew that the guerilla warfare that had worked so well before would not work with an army that size. For what may have been the first time, fear set in.

Before they set off, Abercrombie ordered his men to lighten their weight by shedding some of their clothing. They cut their long coats to jackets and trimmed their hat brims. It not only relieved them from the July heat and gave them less to snag on the brush but also allowed them to move through the water less encumbered. It was effective, and the fleet made it up the lake in surprisingly good time, leaving the fort little time for reinforcements to reach it.

Abercrombie landed about an hour's march from the fort and waited a day before continuing, debating over the best route to take. The delay, seemingly innocuous, was, in reality, incredibly costly.

Montcalm used that day wisely; neither the British nor the French know it, but that day would make all the difference. He knew he was outnumbered five to one and that the small fort would be devastated if the British set up their artillery on the high grounds surrounding it. He had to act quickly. Knowing there was only one road onto the peninsula where the fort stood, he decided that was where they would mount their defense.

He brought his men to the hilltop about a mile from the fort, where they created a maze, using logs and sharpened branches to slow and tangle the enemy.[79] Montcalm was not certain they could win against such overwhelming numbers, but he would try to at least hold out until reinforcements—one thousand regulars and one thousand native warriors—arrived. Those hopes were soon dashed when the British reached him before his reinforcements. It would also be the first time the French fought without their native allies, furthering their disadvantage.

Montcalm also sent out regiments to guard the area where the British landed and the portage roads he was sure they would take. Colonel François-Charles de Bourlamaque was guarding a key bridge over the La Chute River. He burned it and took his men north to meet Montcalm and the main contingent.

The next day, the British began their march toward the fort. Hacking their way through the dense wild undergrowth, Lord Howe took a forward party of Army Rangers headed by Rogers and went ahead of the main detachment in order to check on the French position near the sawmill. Two more disastrous mistakes had just been made.

---

[79] Aptly named Rattlesnake Hill at the time, it is now known as Mount Defiance.

Howe and Rogers were met by a French detachment that was moving through the dense woods looking for them. Not long after the first shot was fired, a bullet found its way toward General Howe. It struck the left side of his chest, piercing his lungs and heart. He fell backward off his horse, dead before he even met the ground.

The Army Rangers, though aware of Howe's demise, held firm and quickly worked to surround the French. Trapped, the French were like fish in a barrel, the British fire decimating their numbers. Less than one hundred men escaped back into the woods.

Despite their victory, the rest of the British army had a difficult time following the example set by the Rangers. After they found out about Howe's death, they were gripped with anxiety and thrown into confusion. As darkness fell over them, the situation worsened. Upon hearing screams coming from the woods, the nervous soldiers fired almost blindly, hitting many of their own with friendly fire. It took hours for Abercrombie and the officers to get their men back under control.

The confusion following the conflict gave the French additional time, time that Montcalm used to his utmost advantage. His men finished the outerworks log maze and took their positions, with each party stationed fifty steps apart along the road to the fort.

On July 8th, Abercrombie prepared to launch the assault. With confidence in Johnson and his four hundred Mohawk warriors, he decided that an offensive was better than a siege. In his haste, the meeting where he gave the officers instructions was hurried, and they left unclear about what exactly they were doing. Only Abercrombie's last words of the meeting rang in their ears. "We must attack in any way, and not waste time in talking or consulting how." That haste and lack of clear planning was another critical error in a string of many.

Abercrombie ordered the cannons on the lake to fire on the fort, but since they were out of range, the bombardment was nothing but a waste of time and munitions. Abercrombie may have been trying to make a show of force or distract or disconcert the enemy as he waited for more cannons to arrive by boat. But little did he know, half of his siege cannons lay at the bottom of the deep lake. Any other artillery they had would never reach them in time.

The rest of the army marched up the hill where the French were taking their stand behind their outerworks maze, with multiple skirmishes breaking out along the way. The British struggled up the hill with their heavy packs, stumbling on branches and stones and breaking the rhythm of their march.

When they got to the top of the hill, Colonel William Haviland led the charge. When the firing began, he mistakenly thought the main assault had begun. Telling his forward militiamen to "fall down," he marched his regulars ahead. It was yet another tragic error for the British. They marched straight into the fire of Montcalm's best marksmen, who were stationed behind the barricades, their guns positioned through narrow slits in the logs. Haviland's men "fell like pigeons."[80]

The rest of the British frontal assault tried to reach the solid log breastwork, but first, they had to navigate the tangled maze of sharpened stakes and branches before it. The sharp stakes snagged their coats and tangled them in the brush, slowing their advance to a crawl. The maze-like barrier forced their well-formed lines to be dispersed. That division made them much easier targets. The French snipers fired from their protected positions, keeping the British from coming near their protective barricade. They were "cut down like grass," the ground "strewn with dead and dying. A man could not stand without being hit. Balls came by the handful."[81]

---

[80] The Mohawks had been left behind on the hill as auxiliaries and scouts while the British regulars marched forward. They watched as the British were mowed down by French guns before they turned and left without joining the fight.

[81] These were the eyewitness words of a Connecticut soldier who fought in the battle.

The French were firing furiously, sending a metallic blizzard of bullets toward the British line. For every three shots the British took, the French were able to answer with five and with more deadly accuracy. The screams of men went up through the woods as they fell, while others cowered behind stumps and boulders. The British commanders were quickly losing control of the army and the situation.

Now the fearsome, almost legendary division of the Scottish Highlanders, known as the Black Watch, launched themselves toward the barricade, their intimidating black tartan a blur.[82] They made it within twenty paces of the barrier, closer than any other regiment, and began a three-hour firefight with the entrenched Frenchman. They were only able to see "their hats and the ends of their muskets." They persisted, though, looking to find any weaknesses in the wall before them. The unceasing and fierce determination of the Black Watch managed to press the French, especially with a move that lived up to their reputation.

Some Black Watch members suddenly ran from the firing line, dodging the flurry of French bullets. They leaped onto the log barricade with terrifying ferocity, appearing like "roaring lions breaking from their chains." Despite their wild courage, those who made it over the wall were cut down by the French, taking the most catastrophic loss of any regiment.

By nightfall, two thousand British laid on the hill, dead or wounded, while those regulars who survived retreated behind the militia-held lines. In contrast, the French lost only 380 men. The British again found out that superior numbers did not necessarily equal victory, and they retreated. They tried to make a run for the lake, but they were slowed, as the thick mud consumed their shoes

---

[82] The Black Watch was a royal regiment named for the black tartan they wore. They were known for their fierce, fearless fighting, which was compared very closely to that of the native warriors. Even the native warriors themselves viewed the Black Watch that way.

and took them right from their feet. The soldiers didn't care; in their frenzy to leave, they didn't even stop to pick up their shoes. Some ran barefoot or with only one shoe on back down the hill.

It was a day of glorious victory for Montcalm and his garrison at the fort. They were sure to see honor for their amazing victory.[83] But Montcalm was not so naïve to think he had seen the last of the British at the fort. The next time, he might not be so fortunate. He pleaded with headquarters for more men and equipment, telling them that "miracles cannot always be expected." However, he would never receive these two essential components.[84] The French Crown wrote back to Montcalm that since France was occupied with the war on the continent, it did not have the resources to send him more men. They told him, "When the house is on fire, one cannot occupy oneself with the stable." Unnerved by the large British showing and unable or unwilling to send help to North America, Paris officials told Montcalm and the French command in Canada to "think only of making peace."

Abercrombie's reputation, on the other hand, was shattered. He felt the scorn of his men as they dejectedly rowed back toward Fort William Henry.[85] The British had all their hopes resting on his ability to win and, in this case, win quickly and decisively. All that was dashed

---

[83] Despite the surprising win, Governor Vaudreuil condemned Montcalm for not chasing after the retreating British and finishing them off. Montcalm, however, would not have his victory disparaged and shot back at the governor, "When I went to war, I did the best I could...when one is not pleased with one's lieutenants, one had better take the field in person."

[84] The French Crown did send Montcalm eight hundred recruits who had no experience and needed to be trained, but what he asked for and needed were experienced regiments. The French king was more concerned with the costly war they were waging in Europe, one that was draining France's finances to the breaking point.

[85] The New England militia began to insultingly refer to Abercrombie as "Mrs. Nabbycrombie." Even the Iroquois warriors joined in with their own disparaging remarks, tauntingly referring to him as "an old squaw [woman]" that should "wear a petticoat."

within eight hours on a muddy hill. But despite the humiliating loss, the British still pressed on toward victory.

Chapter 12 – The British Turn the Tide

The British were understandably angered and humiliated by the events at Fort Carillon. But instead of losing hope, it whipped them into a greater frenzy, making them determined to take Canada "at any cost." The French may have been thinking about peace, but the British were not.

They turned their eyes once again toward Fort Frontenac. Though they hadn't been able to take the fort in a previous attempt, General John Bradstreet suggested that since Abercrombie still had a large number of men under his command, they could be used for a successful strike against the Canadian fort.

It was a bold move—they would have to march the army 250 miles through mountainous wilderness inhabited by the Iroquois. But after their recent loss, they were looking for an easy win. Bradstreet called Frontenac "ripe for the plucking," and they bet on the French not expecting them to attack again so quickly. They hoped this would allow them to take the French by surprise. Their gamble would pay off.

In early August, Abercrombie and Bradstreet gathered 3,600 men, nearly all provincial militiamen, and set off on their difficult journey. The French might not have known that the British were on their way, but they did know that the fort was in dire straits. Almost all of the men garrisoned there had been pulled out to go to Fort Carillon. Only 110 men and 9 small boats remained to defend it. They just hoped that their cannons could prevent the British from making it across the lake should they come.

The trek was arduous for the British militia. Not only was their overland march made difficult by overgrown and uncleared roads, but it was also punctuated by low water in the rivers and creeks that ground their boats in silt. They had to stop and build dams to raise the water levels in order to move their boats. By the time they reached the mouth of the Oswego River on August 21st, 1758, six hundred men had deserted Bradstreet. But they continued to press onward.

The next day, the British boarded several hundred bateaux and set sail across the lake, heading straight for Frontenac. Had the French seen them coming, Bradstreet's fleet might have sustained some damage and given Frontenac a chance. But as fate would have it, the French boats never saw the British coming.

They landed and set up their artillery in secret, the French never suspecting what was coming their way. The next morning, the French were shaken from their beds by artillery fire. The British laid down a sustained barrage, bombarding the walls and trapping the French. The French knew within the first few minutes that they were doomed. They put up the obligatory token resistance in accord with European war etiquette, knowing it was the only way they could surrender with honor.

Within hours, the flag of surrender was raised. The British accorded the soldiers the honors of war and allowed the fort's elderly commander, Pierre-Jacques Payen de Noyen, to return to Montreal. Though the fort was small, it was a major victory for the British in a number of ways. Fort Frontenac was the key to the St. Lawrence

River, which would allow them access to Canada. It was a strategic conquest—the way to Quebec was now wide open.

In addition, the British not only claimed the food, weapons (including sixty cannons), and supplies within the fort—a major windfall for them—but they also took the supplies meant for other French forts in the north, depriving them of critical essentials.[86] This short battle was an enormous and crippling loss for the French—a loss from which they could not recover.

Now that the British had control of the St. Lawrence on the northern end, they wanted to round out their seizure of the important waterway by capturing the southern end as well. The British now had decent control over the Northeast, but they knew that in order to win the west, they had to take the Ohio Forks area, the region that disastrously slipped through their grasp early on in the war. Taking the Ohio Valley meant another attempt at taking the indomitable Fort Duquesne.

Even though it had been three years, the British were wary about the mission, and they were determined not to repeat Braddock's calamitous mistake. They put Scotsman General John Forbes in charge of the mission, and they began to create a plan. Instead of taking Braddock's route through Virginia, Forbes planned to cut a new, more direct path through the dense forests of Pennsylvania. He would have six thousand men at his disposal. As they chopped their way toward Ohio, they would build outpost supply stations for themselves every forty to fifty miles. They did not want to get stuck without necessities in the middle of an unfamiliar wilderness again.

Aside from his logistical plans, the forward-thinking Forbes realized he needed to do something that Braddock or any other British commander had done before. He knew that what Washington had been saying, that they needed native allies, was true. And he

---

[86] Eight hundred thousand livres' worth of provisions was captured, equal to more than $1.07 million today, making it quite a windfall for the British.

needed a diplomatic envoy to actively woo the Delaware, Shawnee, and other Pennsylvania tribes. Without them, victory was all but hopeless.

Forbes enlisted the help of Delaware-speaking Christian missionary Christian Frederick Post, who had his work cut out for him. Post was determined to win the natives away from the French, and he held a multi-day council with several tribal chiefs, the most prominent among these being Teedyuscung, the self-styled "king of the Delaware." Post told the natives that the British wanted peace with the tribes and promised they weren't there to take their land but to drive the French out. But given the history of the British breaking promises, stealing land, and defrauding the native tribes, they were understandably doubtful about their claims.[87]

Post would have to overcome decades of rightful and justified animosity toward the British, who the natives believed had taken land that was their birthright and inheritance. He asked the chiefs to lay down their hatchet and form a treaty, promising that things would be different this time. He agreed that the British would not settle west of the Allegheny Mountains and would ensure the tribes had thousands of acres of land for themselves. After nineteen days, the chiefs finally agreed to the alliance—they knew they needed the British in order to keep their lands. However, they wanted the British to know that they were a power to be reckoned with and that they could make peace as well as break it if the promises were not upheld. Post agreed to bring their warning back to British command, though he knew all too well it was likely to fall on deaf ears. The British only cared that they now had the allies they sorely needed.

While the British were making treaties with the Native Americans, the French were losing their allies. Governor Vaudreuil knew that their native allies didn't truly fight for France; they fought for

---

[87] One of the most outrageous examples of this was the 1686 Walking Land Purchase, an agreement made by William Penn and the Delaware. The vague terms originally laid out led to an egregious abuse of the agreement by the British in 1737.

themselves and the land that was theirs. However, he also knew that he needed to retain their loyalty. It was the only hope for winning.

However, his retention of native allies came across three serious obstacles. First, Montcalm had been resistant to accepting help from the tribes. He was a staunch believer in fighting by the European battle etiquette and detested the "savage" battle tactics, which he found distastefully brutal. The second major issue was that the French no longer had what they needed to keep their native allies. With the supplies stored at Fort Frontenac now in the hands of the delighted British, the French had no gifts of guns or other goods to woo them. Without incentives, the natives would hardly look their way. The third problem lay within the native community itself. The war had taken a heavy toll on them. Smallpox brought by the Europeans, as well as hunger and warfare, had decimated their populations. In some places, entire villages had been wiped out. They were tired of war and had little more to give to this white man's conflict.

Issues with native allies weren't the only big obstacles that made Montcalm nervous. Like Fort Frontenac, Fort Duquesne was now weakly defended because the men garrisoned there were sent to fight on the Canadian front. Since the fort was in such an isolated location, it would be difficult to get enough men, munitions, and supplies to the fort to bring it back to its former strength.

But it was not just Duquesne that the French couldn't supply; the Frontenac debacle had deprived them of supplies for all their other forts. This problem was further exacerbated by corruption among the French, with sorely needed money being gambled or frittered away by the authorities. As a consequence, the French army was facing serious hunger. Montcalm was enraged. How could his men be expected to fight and fight courageously at that while weak and demoralized from hunger? Montcalm knew they were in trouble.

While Montcalm was anxiously trying to keep his army supplied and retain their native allies, Forbes and his men were chopping their way through the dense virgin forests of Pennsylvania—much to the chagrin of George Washington.[88] Washington was eager to return to finish what he had started in the Ohio Valley, so he joined Forbes. When Forbes showed him the route he wanted to cut, Washington insisted that Braddock's previous road was the better way to go. The two locked horns. When Forbes got his hands on a letter George Washington had written to another officer bemoaning Forbes's decision, he was angered, believing Washington to be a fool. The feeling was certainly mutual. Washington eventually lost this argument with Forbes, as well as his good relationship with the general.

When Forbes and his men were within fifty miles of Duquesne, they put the finishing touches on their last outpost, Loyal Hannon. It would be the key staging area to launch their assault. Scouts stealthily snuck out to high vantage points to try to find out just how strong the French force was.

The French, who were almost always in the know about the whereabouts of the British, resorted to their old tricks. They sent out raiding parties to ambush and harass the British as they worked and hunted in the woods. Men often returned to camp bloodied and battered from surprise attacks, and inevitably, this began to unnerve the rest of the men.

However, the British were tired of the guerilla tactics used by the French and native warriors, so they decided to strike back. Major James Grant, a Highlander, proposed a bold plan to give the French a taste of their own medicine under the guise of a reconnaissance mission near the fort. However, he planned to take five hundred men with him—far too many for reconnaissance. It was fairly obvious that Grant had something up his sleeve.

Grant obviously had too few men for an all-out assault, but he knew that the French fort was weakly defended. With this knowledge, as well as his thirst for fame and glory, he wanted to make a secret bid

---

[88] The route they cut still exists today; it is now the modern-day Pennsylvania Turnpike.

to take Duquesne himself. Could he and his men possibly pull off such an ambitious plan?

Lieutenant Colonel Henry Bouquet encouraged Grant's audacious plan, giving him an additional 250 men. On September 14th, Grant set off and easily marched to within a mile of the fort. Grant's men then split into three units, and they confidently began their final march, bagpipes blasting the air and announcing their position. However, it didn't matter how much noise they made; the French already knew where they were, thanks to their native scouts. And the French were right there waiting for them. Fort commander François-Marie de Lignery, a battle-hardened marine, was no fool. He quickly went out with some troops and warriors and set a trap. And when the British advanced, the trap was sprung. Lignery's men swooped down on the surprised British and routed them. Three hundred of Grant's men were killed, and Grant himself was taken prisoner and quickly shipped to Montreal. Forbes, whose health was severely deteriorating due to dysentery, reeled under the heavy blow of the defeat and called Grant's actions rash.

The quick victory, however, did not change the dire situation Lignery and the fort were facing. With no way to get supplies, they were running out of food. Emboldened by his victory and motivated by desperation, Lignery shortly thereafter decided to launch an assault on Loyal Hannon, hoping to raid its storehouses.

They made three attempts at the outpost during the day but were beaten back every time. Lignery made one last attempt at night and managed to pick off some sentries but failed to breach the station. He and his men were forced to return to the fort, hungry and provisionless as ever. Despite their lack of success, the thought of facing starvation as winter approached was a strong incentive for Lignery to continue his attempts. For ten days, the French desperately tried to reach the British stockpiles, failing each time.

After the French attempted once again to steal horses and livestock, the British had had enough. Forbes sent Mercer to strike back in a woodland battle as the French again approached. However, once they engaged the French in battle, Mercer's provincials had difficulty attaining a victory. Forbes quickly sent Washington and his Virginia regiment to help Mercer.

Washington and his men approached the battle near dusk, the darkened light combined with powder smoke and fog making it difficult to see. Shadowy figures passed through the gray air, and the sparks of musket fire created brief flashes of brightness. Washington and his men fired toward the indistinct figures and flashes.

One of Mercer's officers, Captain Thomas Bullitt, saw the new volley of fire coming toward them, and he quickly realized what was happening. He ran straight toward the muskets of the Virginia regiment, screaming for them to halt their fire. The Virginians were firing straight into Mercer's regiment! Washington heard Bullitt, and he also stepped between the lines in an effort to halt their fire, even using his sword to push firing muskets up toward the sky.

When the firing stopped and the smoke began to clear, the gravity of the situation became obvious. Washington's horror mounted as they saw fourteen of their own dead on the ground, with another twenty-six wounded, all by friendly fire. Bullitt was incensed by Washington's carelessness. He blamed Washington for the incident and would never forgive him for it. Washington, however, somewhat spooked by his near-death experience, believed that divine providence had spared him for something greater.

As terrible as the blunder of the skirmish was, there was a bright spot. When the French ran from the fray, they left three of their men behind. The British took them as prisoners and pressed them for information about the fort. The information they dug up was pure gold. According to the prisoners, Fort Duquesne was weakly defended. It was so weakly defended, in fact, that the commanders were thinking of abandoning it. Forbes was overjoyed at the news. Now was the time to strike.

Within two weeks, Forbes was ready to mount his final assault. The British were so close to their goal, but Washington inexplicably started to press Forbes to abandon the plan and return to Braddock's already-cut road. The idea was ridiculous, and with provincial enlistments due to be up in a few days, Forbes was determined to press on.

French anxiety had grown, and they had finally come to terms with the fact that their situation was utterly hopeless. On November 18th, 2,500 of Forbes's men were marching toward the fort. There was no way Lignery's forces could repel them. Even their native allies had packed up and left the fort. It would be a complete rout.

Lignery ordered the evacuation of two hundred men to other outposts while the rest set charges around the fort. Now was not the time to worry about putting up symbolic resistance and being accorded the honors of war. After what had happened at Fort Frontenac, they wanted to leave nothing for the British but a pile of smoldering rubble.

When the British came within view of the fort, there was no army waiting to greet them—only an abandoned fort burning along the river. Forbes won the Ohio Forks without a shot, but he wouldn't have the security of the fort to spend the winter.[89] Leaving some men behind to rebuild it, he took the rest of his men back to Philadelphia.[90,91]

---

[89] Before Forbes left, he renamed the area Pittsborough, now known as Pittsburgh.

[90] Forbes would never live to see the rebuilding of the fort or enjoy the British victory of the area. He died from poor health just a few weeks later.

[91] Afterward, Washington took some men and returned to the battlefield of Braddock's disastrous defeat. The remains of their dead fellow soldiers were never claimed or buried; they had been left to nature and the elements those past three years. Washington had them buried with the military honors they were accorded. He then returned to Mount Vernon, once again retiring from military life and starting his new life by marrying Martha Custis.

By the end of 1758, the British, despite many mistakes, had turned things around. But in truth, they had not done it alone. Without the Iroquois, who had given up their fifty-year policy of neutrality, as well as the other tribes who abandoned the French and came to their side, things might have turned out very differently for the British. However, just because things were looking up for the British didn't mean they had won the war just yet.

Chapter 13 – The Fall of Quebec and the "End" of the True Canada

It was late July 1759, and Colonel James Wolfe paced the ground on the Île d'Orléans on the St. Lawrence River. After having received "secret instructions" from the king regarding a three-pronged attack centered in and near Canada, his journey north was difficult. He battled near-constant seasickness and braved an unusually severe winter, and he now found himself facing the core of the French forces.

He was anxious to take some real action against Quebec. The British had been successful in their other two campaigns. If Wolfe could pull it off, this would be the final and decisive battle in accomplishing their goal.

Only a few days earlier, William Johnson had taken one thousand British soldiers and a large contingent of native warriors against Fort Niagara. The French, who had only five hundred men at the fort and had lost the majority of their native allies, were at a disadvantage from the get-go. As French reinforcements made their way to rescue the fort, nineteen-year-old British army officer Joseph Brant was eager for the attack.[92] He and his men pulled a page out of the French playbook and ambushed the French as they marched out of the dense forest. The French took heavy casualties, the worst of these being the mortal wounding of the fort's commander. With their help neutralized, the fort was doomed, and they had no choice but to surrender.

Around the same time, the British returned to the site of one of their greatest humiliations—Fort Carillon. Knowing the British were coming with another large force of eleven thousand men, including that thorn in their side Captain Rogers and his Rangers, the French didn't believe that their good fortune would hold out a second time. They evacuated the fort, leaving only four hundred men behind to "take care" of the fort.

As the British dug siege trenches toward the fort, the French were turning their cannons toward their own walls, laying mines, and making a trail of gunpowder that led straight to their munitions storehouse. If the British wanted to take the fort, the French were going to give them an explosive surprise. The departing French quickly took torches and set the long fuses on fire before running.

The British caught a few French who were fleeing, and they informed the British that the fort was about to blow. British commanders wanted to save the fort at all costs and offered a king's ransom to anyone who would douse the fuses. But the British soldiers knew that those one hundred guineas would do them no good if they were blown to pieces.

That night, as darkness set in, the ground suddenly shook with a tremendous boom, and the sky suddenly lit up with a large explosion, the French flag still flying above the burning fort. Though the outer stone walls of the fort held up, the interior burned for two days. It was

---

[92] Brant (also known as Thayendanegea), a Mohawk officer in the British army, later became a tribal chief. (He was reportedly the great-grandson of King Hendrick.) He also acted as a liaison in efforts to bridge the gap between the white man's world and the Six Nations. He was also reportedly involved in two massacres, earning him the nickname "Monster Brant."

a tremendous victory for the British. Along with nearby Fort Crown Point,[93] the British controlled the Lake George/Lake Champlain region, allowing General Jeffery Amherst a clear path toward Wolfe and his men and Canada.[94]

Wolfe must have been encouraged by the British victories to his south. He only had 8,500 men, which was less than the 12,000 he had requested, but they were well-trained. They had faced skirmishes with Montcalm's sixteen thousand soldiers, but Wolfe was not concerned about the superior numbers of French soldiers. He wrote to his mother, telling her that Montcalm was "at the head of a great number of bad soldiers, and I am at the head of a small number of good ones."

But no matter how good his soldiers were, they had not made any headway against the impenetrable city. It sat safely in the high cliffs on the other side of the river, nearly impervious to a frontal water-born assault. Wolfe desperately looked for any "opportunity to strike a blow" on his enemy.

Montcalm, on the other hand, remained "entrenched up to the chin" within the city, refusing to be drawn out into a battle he would surely lose. That's not to say Wolfe didn't try his hardest to shake them out of their secure city fortress. But Montcalm wasn't falling for any of Wolfe's tactics. He knew that as long as the British could not get them outside the city and draw them into open battle, they had a chance. They would try to outwait the enemy, hoping to hold on until winter could drive them away.

Though Montcalm decided to concentrate his manpower on holding Quebec, he was no fool—he saw the writing on the wall for North America and the French. Eerily, he had predicted earlier in the year that "Canada will fall during the upcoming campaign season."

---

[93] This was built on the site of the conquered Fort Saint-Frédéric.

[94] The British rebuilt the fort and renamed it Fort Ticonderoga (from the Iroquois word meaning "between two waters") and held it until 1775 when it was taken by colonial Americans under Ethan Allen and Benedict Arnold.

And now the fulfillment of that prediction was staring at him from across the river.

Wolfe knew that even though Montcalm could wait it out within the city, time was ticking for him. Winter, which started early in Canada, was just over the horizon. If Wolfe was going to help bring North America under the control of the British that year, he was going to have to make some dramatic moves. Day after day, his cannons and mortars bombarded its walls, and day after day, they crumbled a bit more as the French scrambled to keep them intact. But despite the growing pile of rubble around the city, it was still not enough to win.

Boarding the HMS *Russell* on July 31ˢᵗ, 1759, Wolfe, along with men on two other war vessels, surreptitiously made their way up the river under cover of darkness. They crossed the river to the area near Montmorency Falls, hoping to get a better view of French activities. Wolfe also had another plan in mind—attack the temporary French fortifications protecting the northern side of the city. He hoped to flush the French from their entrenched positions. Once they were out in the open, the British would have a clear line of fire into their ranks. What Wolfe hadn't realized until he landed was that from high on the hill, the French guns on the walls of Quebec could reach him and his men before they even made it to their redoubt.[95] That would make Wolfe's plan far riskier. He and his men would be caught in the open between two unreachable French defensive lines. Wolfe decided to go ahead with his plan anyway.

As he waited for the main body of his landing forces to arrive, Wolfe could see dire problems already brewing. The ships carrying his troops became grounded on the river's shoals, preventing them from reaching Wolfe. By the time they were able to get themselves loose and find another landing spot, the storm clouds had already begun to gather.

---

[95] Temporary fortification or defensive structure.

As Wolfe and his men finally advanced toward the redoubt, the French troops watched them from the hill. It must have been quite amusing to the soldiers who had fought outside Fort Carillon to see the British making yet another foolish attempt. They laid down withering fire, a rain of bullets from the French hill pummeling the British ranks.

The French assault slowed their advance, but it did not stop them. And it might not have stopped them if it had not been for the intervention of Mother Nature. Just a short while after the firing began, rain from the sky poured down on the British, wetting their gunpowder. With their weapons unable to fire, they were as good as unarmed. Wolfe had taken heavy losses in a short amount of time, and he was forced to retreat across the mudflats in a confused, angry, and exhausted escape. Angry that he had persisted in such an ill-advised assault, he wrote, "Many excellent officers were hurt in this foolish business."

Although the French were victorious, Montcalm could not celebrate. He knew that the British would not give up when they were so close to their goal. He wrote to the French Crown, begging the king to send him reinforcements; otherwise, he could not hold the region for France. The reply he received was disappointing, to say the least. The king told him that he would not send more troops but instead sent his compliments, flattering Montcalm by saying he relied on the commander's zeal and knowledge to save Canada.

Montcalm was right about Wolfe; he did not even consider giving up. Instead, he continued to find ways to try to draw the French out into battle. Propelled by anger over his loss, the inability to conquer Quebec, and the insults the French had afforded the British, Wolfe and his men began burning everything they could reach on the other side of the river. The settlements and smaller towns outside the city bore the brunt of this rage, as 1,400 homes were turned to ash.

Wolfe also maneuvered some of his warships upriver. If he could not get to Quebec, maybe an attack on Montreal would anger the French into engaging in an open battle. British siege guns bombarded the city, setting it ablaze. Terrifying infernos raged, creating horrors this war had not seen before, especially for the many non-combatant refugees who had sought safety in the city. Montcalm, though shaken, refused to budge.

By September, Wolfe was in a desperate state in more ways than one. One-third of his army was incapacitated by illness, and Wolfe himself was gravely ill with fever and chronic maladies. He believed he wouldn't survive much longer, and it would be a disgrace to die without gaining Quebec. Despite his illness, he was highly motivated to form an audacious plan to attack the city.

On September 12th, Wolfe's plan went into action. Part of the British fleet sailed down the river and began to attack the city of Beauport. They hoped that the French would believe it was just another small conflict but large enough to distract them from what the British were really planning.

As the bombardment commenced, 4,500 men rowed across the river to the base of the cliffs named Anse-au-Foulon. They were going to scale the cliffs in the dark. The first troops up greeted the sentries in French. Believing that the men were French reserves, the sentries let down their guard. The British soldiers easily captured the bewildered guards and opened the way for the rest of the regiments to safely climb the cliffs. Within five hours, the British had scaled the cliffs and positioned themselves on the Plains of Abraham. When sunlight began to dawn, Montcalm was shocked. He saw the red coats of the British dotted across the field on the more exposed western side of the city. Wolfe's plan worked—to Montcalm, it was as if they had appeared out of nowhere.

Despite Montcalm's firm stance of not meeting the British out in the open, he saw something unusual that would inevitably cause him to change his mind. He was well aware that the British regulars were superior to his French militiamen, but he noticed that Wolfe had spread his men into two ranks instead of three—something Montcalm had never seen before. This formation caused the British to be spread out across the battlefield in a thin line. To Montcalm, this seemed to him to be a breach-able weakness.

Montcalm believed that he would only need one column to defeat the British, and he and his men marched out to the field. The two empires would meet in the classic European battle formation that Montcalm so loved. But as the not-so-disciplined French militiamen marched out of the city to meet them, things quickly began to fall apart.

Unable to keep their lines, the French began firing at the British. The Redcoats held fast, and not one of them fell to the ground—the French had begun firing before their guns were even in range, wasting valuable time and ammunition. The British did not even flinch, and they continued to stare down the blue coats of the advancing French forces. If this first volley was any indication of the state of French training, the British could remain confident in their fight.

The French continued their advance, but before they could position themselves, the British were ready for them. With two musket balls loaded at a time, the Redcoats decimated the French line. The field was quickly littered in blue.[96] In less than ten minutes, the surviving French fled back to the city, leaving 1,500 dead on the plains. It was clear that Montcalm was right all along—they were no match for the British in an open battle.

However, it no longer mattered how right Montcalm was. He had made a fatal error, and it would be his last. He was shot in the abdomen, the red blood stains spreading through his white undercoat as he was rushed to a physician's house. It was too late; he could not be saved. His end, however, was less dramatic or heroic than Wolfe's.

---

[96] Later, British historian Sir John Fortescue called the action "the most perfect volley ever fired on a battlefield."

Wolfe took musket fire to his wrist and chest during the battle, and his men found him lying on the field. They quickly rushed to find a physician to save him, but he refused the help. He knew his body was too weakened by sickness and that he could not survive the mortal wounds. He bravely told his men that his end had come. However, he told them that he could die knowing that he had been a hero and that his name would be known all over the British Empire.

The French returned to the city utterly demoralized. Their fierce leader was dead, the city was in near ruins, and desertion from the army was rampant. With food and supplies running low, it seemed impossible that they could wait out a siege inside the city until the bitter winter winds brought them release. They knew another assault by the British would only lead to more unimaginable carnage. Four days after this decisive battle, the French had no choice but to surrender.

Such a climactic battle ending in the dramatic deaths of both brilliant commanders seemed like it would bring a decisive end to this war of two empires. Yet, it would rage on for another year. Peace had fled all of Europe since war raged there as well, and peace also remained the last thing on the mind of General Amherst. Despite their incredible conquest of Quebec, Amherst would not rest until the British had taken all of Canada.

By the summer of 1760, Amherst was hellbent on taking the last French holdout—Montreal. The way there, though, was fraught with danger. He and his men would have to navigate the dangerous rapids rushing down the St. Lawrence River, and if they made it, they would still have to survive the gauntlet of French-allied Canadian Mohawk territory. In early August, he set off from Fort Oswego with an army of 10,000 men and 750 native warriors.

Amherst knew the Mohawks were his greatest weakness and the greatest strength of the French. In order to win, he needed to get rid of this threat, which he referred to as the "enemy's Indian scoundrels."[97] Amherst despised his own Iroquois allies, calling them the "savage enemy," but he knew he needed them to win. He also knew he would need diplomatic tactics to neutralize the Mohawk problem.

As Amherst and his forces made their way up the St. Lawrence River, they took the time to stop at various Mohawk villages. The British worked to convince the Mohawk chiefs that they just wanted peace with them and did not want to fight if it could be helped. Amherst's plan worked. The Mohawk agreed to stay out of the fight. Once again, the French lost one of their most valuable assets: native allies.

With the native "problem" peacefully taken care of, Amherst could now turn to organize his massive offensive against Montreal. Three British armies converged to finish this fight in Canada, creating an impressive and terrifying force that would come up against the city all at once.

On September 8th, 1760, the French in Montreal saw a crushing force of Redcoats at their doorstep. Not wanting a repeat of the previous year, they surrendered without a shot being fired. Though the surrender was bloodless, the French suffered the insult of not being allowed to take their regimental flags. The British wanted to twist the knife and take their flags as trophies. The French burned

---

[97] In a quest for vengeance against the Abenaki the November before, Amherst sent out Rogers and a unit of his Rangers on an ill-fated revenge mission. Although Rogers "successfully" attacked one of their villages, he and his men were chased by the French and Abenaki into a nightmarish retreat. Sick, weak, and starving, the Rangers eventually resorted to roasting their own shoes and powder horns for food. Some even turned to cannibalism, eating their own fallen compatriots. Many Rangers were lost on the return from the mission. Amherst's vengeance cost his men dearly and earned him virtually nothing.

them, preferring to turn their flags to ashes rather than see them in the hands of the gloating British army.

A week after Montreal surrendered, Robert Rogers, now a major, captured Fort Detroit for the British. With that, the French and Indian War was essentially over. However, the problems for the British were just beginning.

Conclusion

The British may have won North America, but the question was could they rule it?

The American colonists, who had willingly sacrificed men and money to the war, were disenchanted with British Parliament on the other side of the ocean. They believed that their efforts during the war should give them certain rights, specifically the right to be free from taxation by the Crown and to levy their own taxes through their own representatives.

Britain's wars were costly. By the end of the Seven Years' War, its national debt had doubled. It tried to recoup some of its money through what the colonists viewed as oppressive taxation. Since their bitterness had been brewing against their mother country for some time, the tax issue began to push them over the edge. It would spiral into a problem that the British would not be able to contain.

With the Seven Years' War still raging for another three years, Britain needed to send its soldiers from North America to the French-controlled West Indies, as well as Europe, West Africa, and Asia, to fight their war on new ground. In Austria, they would fight for control of northern Europe; in Africa, they would fight over control of the slave trade; and in India, they would fight for a stake in Asia. They fought because a historical empire was on the line, the likes of which had not been seen since Rome ruled the Western world.

In French Canada, British influence took a firm hold over the next century. It made the loss for French Canadians more than just losing their land and forts; they viewed it as a tragic loss of their culture as well. This caused some over the centuries to consider the day Quebec fell as the day "true" Canadian history ended. A few decades later, in "revenge" for Montcalm's death, the French would reemerge as important players in the new American history that began to unfold.

In North America, Amherst's contempt for the native people continued to grow, and it became more than just insulting words. He shunned any overtures of friendship and insulted the natives by refusing to stick with the long-standing customs that their people had shared. He would no longer give them weapons, ammunition, liquor, or any other gifts in an effort to retain peace.

William Johnson, who was serving as a liaison to the First Nations, was alarmed by Amherst's callousness toward their former allies. He knew that if relationships broke down, war would be inevitable—and it would be a war the British could ill-afford to wage. It was not just France that had suffered from the war; Britain had also faced severe financial losses, and there would be far worse long-term consequences to come.

As Amherst began to change the relationship with the native people, from one of powerful allies to that of subjects, the tribes began to balk at the attempts to subjugate them, as well as the further encroachment on their land. Almost as soon as they had made the treaty agreeing to not build west of the Allegheny Mountains, the British broke their promise. The tribes could see where things were headed, and they were very wary of the British, especially after having lost their French allies.

Johnson warned Amherst that continuing on this course would lead to war, but Amherst ignored his concerns. Convinced that the Native Americans were dangerous savages, Amherst knew the British must show their superior power and keep them in subjugation. By 1763, the situation had deteriorated.

In February 1763, the British signed the treaties of Paris and Hubertusburg, ending the Seven Years' War. However, peace in North America continued to elude them. That same year, Ottawa Chief Pontiac gathered a council of tribes to talk about the growing British threat. He told them he had a divine vision where the Creator spoke to him and told him that the land was created for the native people and no one else. Pontiac then called his people to take action to preserve their rights. He further motivated them by saying that his divine vision instructed him to go to war with the British and drive them from their lands. The tribal chiefs agreed to ally to start a war against the British. Tribes that had previously fought each other for many years now agreed to come together for this common cause.

For the British, a new war began while a colonial revolution loomed on the horizon.

Here's another book by Captivating History that you might like

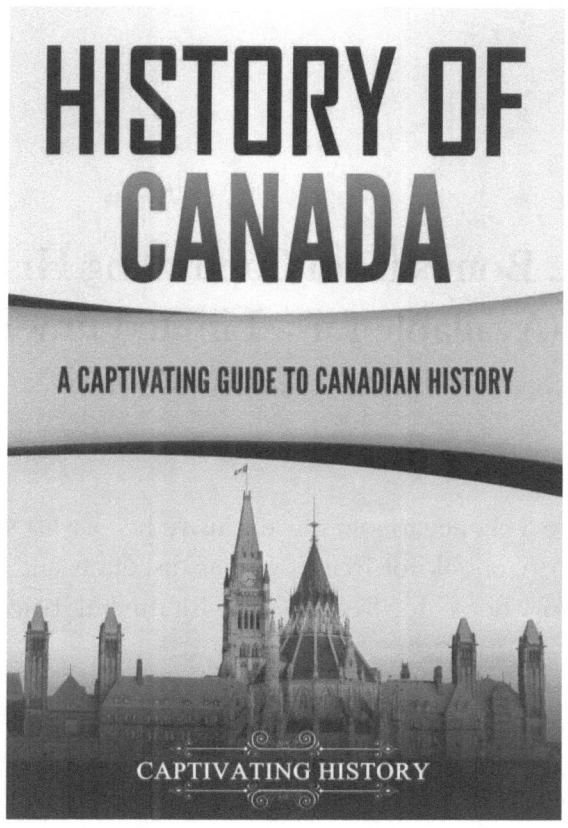

Free Bonus from Captivating History (Available for a Limited time)

Hi History Lovers!

Now you have a chance to join our exclusive history list so you can get your first history ebook for free as well as discounts and a potential to get more history books for free! Simply visit the link below to join.

Captivatinghistory.com/ebook

Also, make sure to follow us on Facebook, Twitter and Youtube by searching for Captivating History.

References

Becky Little. "How 22-Year-Old George Washington Inadvertently Sparked a World War."

https://www.history.com/news/george-washington-french-indian-war-jumonville. Accessed November 1, 2021.

Freeman, Douglas Southall. (1948) *George Washington: A Biography*. New York: Scribner

Stull, Charlene. "Washington's Mission to Fort Le Boeuf."

http://paheritage.wpengine.com/article/washington-mission-fort-le-boeuf/. Accessed November 10, 2021

"Washington and the French & Indian War." https://www.mountvernon.org/george-washington/french-indian-war/washington-and-the-french-indian-war/#_ftn17

Library of Congress. "George Washington's map, accompanying his 'journal to the Ohio,' 1754." https://www.loc.gov/resource/g3820.ct000361/?r=-0.251,0.291,1.605,0.647,0

Parkman, Francis. (1910). *Montcalm and Wolfe (Vol.1)*.

Lengel, Edward G. (2005). *General George Washington: A Military Life*. Random House.

Fowler, William. (2005). *Empires at War*. Walker & Company.

Axelrod, Alan. (2011). *A Savage Empire: Trappers, Traders, Tribes, and the Wars That Made America*. New York: St. Martin's Press.

Green, Karl R. (2002). *The French and Indian War*. Berkeley Heights, NJ: MyReportLinks.com Books.

Gard, Carolyn. (2004). *The French and Indian War: A Primary Source History of the Fight for Territory in North America*. New York: Rosen Central Primary Source.

"Braddock's Defeat." https://www.britishbattles.com/french-indian-war/general-braddocks-defeat-on-the-monongahela-in-1755-part-x/. Accessed November 12, 2012

Hannings, Bud. (2011). *The French and Indian War: A Complete Chronology*. Jefferson, North Carolina: McFarland & Company, Inc., Publishers.

"History of Roger's Island." https://www.rogersisland.org/Rogers%20Island.htm.

Accessed November 15, 2021

November 14, 2021

"Fort William Henry, 1757: A Massacre of Misunderstanding."

https://warfarehistorynetwork.com/2016/01/11/fort-william-henry-1757-a-massacre-of-misunderstanding/ November 15, 2021

David R. Starbuck. "The Massacre at Fort William Henry."

https://www.penn.museum/sites/expedition/the-massacre-at-fort-william-henry/ November 15, 2021

"The Battle of Rogers' Rock."

http://nyindependencetrail.org/stories-Battle-of-Rogers-Rock.html November 20, 2021

Dr. Joseph F. Meany Jr. "Frigid Fury: The Battle on Snowshoes, March 1758."

https://museum.dmna.ny.gov/unit-history/conflict/revolutionary-war-1775-1783/frigid-fury-battle-snowshoes-march-1758 November 20, 2021

Photo: Fort Louisbourg during siege 1758 By Pierre-Charles Canot –

http://collections.britishart.yale.edu/vufind/Record/3628336http://b03.deliver.odai.yale.edu/88/28/88283354-6eee-48bb-ac8f-da6b76d74d5d/ba-obj-47548-0001-pub-large.jpg, Public Domain,

https://commons.wikimedia.org/w/index.php?curid=56023137 November 21, 2021

Stacey, Charles Perry. (1973). *Quebec, 1759: The Siege and the Battle.* London: Pan Books.

"Battle of Quebec, 1759." https://www.britishbattles.com/french-indian-war/battle-of-quebec-1759/. Accessed November 22, 2021

"French & Indian War: North American History." https://www.britannica.com/event/French-and-Indian-War. Accessed November 22, 2021

Made in United States
Troutdale, OR
04/11/2025